Cook Your Way to Love & Harmony

Agus & Frida

Hi, Pa!

looking up to heaven and waves

Hi, Moms!

Yay, we've finally done it.

To those who are going to be inspired by our story

and will start cooking for loved ones: Have Fun!

To other home cooks: May the Love be with Us Always!

Contents

CHAPTER I

The First Love Omelette

THIS IS A BOOK ABOUT LOVE.

It is also a book about cooking good food…

Love and food and how they express each other through cooking. How we can cook food to express our love, and in so doing, how love and food can become one. And by this expression and becoming one, love and food then become part of *us*.

Together, they have power—the power to express our humanity, our love for humanity, and yes, our love for each other.

Love is the greatest gift ever given to humankind. The ability to love is the one thing that sets people apart from all other creatures. It allows us to forge bonds with others not seen anywhere else on earth.

Love can move mountains and love can part oceans, and with it, love allows us to have unbelievable experiences in an otherwise meaningless existence. It is my honest belief—and it has been my experience—that everything accomplished in the world is driven by love in one way or another. Whether it is love for our parents, love for our family, love for our children, or love for our fellow person, nothing has ever been accomplished without love for others as the motivational force.

I remember very well how love shaped my childhood. There was my mother's love, expressed best when she supported me in all I did or tried to do. I remember her sitting on the floor of our modest home, building towers of blocks; or fashioning me a cape or a sword—whatever it was that my childhood fantasies required. Sometimes it was just a hug or a kind word that she had for me, but that was enough.

And then there was my father's love, expressed through his cooking for me.

I remember, a time when I was four years old and had become a very picky eater.

"He is too small, too thin!" my mother said. "He must eat!"

But I scrunched up my nose at every meal, pushing food around on my plate. I clamped my lips shut and, though I loved my mother very much, I would not eat what she had prepared. It was grown-up food, undesirable to me in taste, scent, and texture.

I sustained myself with bites of fruit and bread and especially loved crunchy tidbits like Cheetos and Chitato, junk food that particularly worried my mother.

"He must eat a meal, a *real meal!*" she wailed frequently. "His brain will not grow if he does not *eat!*"

I scrunched my small face and pressed my lips even harder together at mealtimes. Frustrated, my mother would often excuse herself to tend to my baby sister in the bedroom. But my father, he stayed.

And one day, he said, "I know what to do."

My father smiled. He was always smiling at me, no matter how naughty I was—and I often misbehaved in those days.

On that day, as he left the dining hall in our home for the kitchen, I ran from the large, round dining room table, through the small living area, to the yellow door that led to my father's shop. I often peeked through that door, smelling the aromas from neighbourhood restaurants and food stalls and watching the cars pass by. I imagined myself hitching a ride in one of the passing vehicles, riding to somewhere where they would not make me eat proper meals, somewhere I could nibble fruit and bread and eat all the Chitato I wanted. A nice, heavenly garden, with cool breezes and no proper meals with which to be bothered.

And then a new scent wafted out to me, interrupting my dreams of escape. A glorious scent, coming from my own kitchen! It was warm and aromatic, sweet and slightly salty. My stomach rumbled.

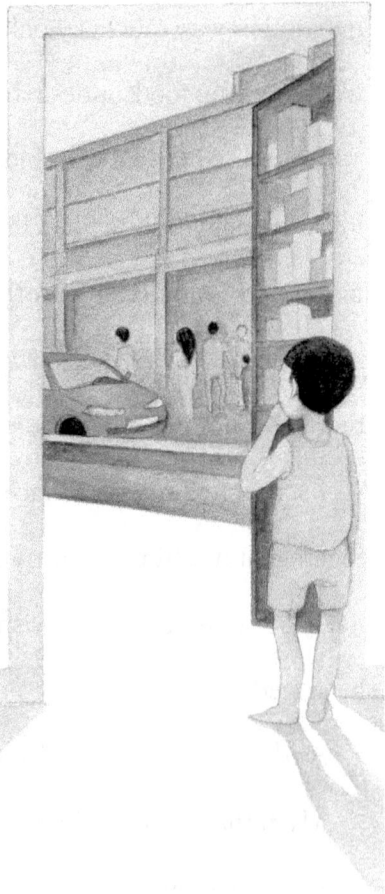

I ran back inside and through the dining hall to the kitchen where my father stood at the stove, cooking. He wore the short pants and short-sleeved shirt that he always wore while cooking. Although quiet, his body nearly hummed with joy for his task— to cook me the perfect meal.

Hearing me, he looked over his broad shoulder and smiled. He removed a frying pan from the stove and said, "Come, Gus. Grab a plate and come with me to the table. I have prepared something special, *just for you.*"

Curious—and interested in the smell of what he had made just for me—I brought a plate back to the dining hall. I sat. My father towered over me, still smiling. Leaning close, he slid something from his frying pan to my plate.

One chicken egg, scrambled and shaped, seasoned with salt. A simple omelette.

I ate that meal with gusto and, as I ate, my mother reappeared with my baby sister on her hip. Ma looked at Pa, and he at her. They grinned. I was eating!

I began to look forward to mealtimes instead of dreading them. My heart would thump with anticipation as soon as I smelled my father's cooking, still the same, simple love omelette. My father began to add some rice and sweet soy sauce to my omelette meal. Growing up in Central Java, Indonesia, this sweet sauce is always the best condiment.

My father knew that by creating a sweet omelette for me out of love, I would not only eat, but I would also have a childhood filled with sweetness and love. He was right.

As time passed, I grew in brain and body from eating the love omelette my father had created for me, but when I was about six years old, my parents—especially my mother, who worried about me often—became anxious because I would not eat vegetables. I was hooked on the sweet omelette and soy sauce, the soft rice. I feared that vegetables were too bitter for my tender taste buds. Once again, my father tapped his head. He had another idea.

This time I did not run from the dining hall but rather followed my father to the kitchen where I watched him as he chopped shallots and spring onion and added these to my omelette.

"Pa, no!" I said, worried that my sweet omelette would be ruined.

"Gus, do you trust me?" he asked.

I looked up into his soft brown eyes, crinkling with the smile he always had for me, and I thought, *I do. I do trust you, Pa.*

So I tried the new omelette, and my father was right! I now had a new, favourite food.

I liked the new omelette so much, I begged my father, "Please, Pa, let me cook it!"

Really, I wanted to cheat. I liked the flavour of the omelette but not the look of the pieces of green in it. I thought if I could chop the onions myself, I would make them disappear. No more green.

My father, big-boned and slightly fat, crossed his large arms and grinned. He was on to me.

"I'll teach you how to cook when the time is right," he said.

"Aww, Pa, when will that be?" I asked, lowering my eyes and kicking at the floor with my toes.

"When you are ready, the time will be right," he said, which made no sense to me, but he was my father and I did not argue.

Month after month, year after year, I grew and was soon tall enough to stand next to my father and watch him chop vegetables and cook. Many times, I insisted that it was my time to learn, and many times he shook his head, refusing me with a smile. I scowled and crossed my arms over my chest in anger, but he would not budge on this.

When I was about ten years old, my father changed the recipe of my omelette again. After smashing red chilli and garlic into a puree, he added it to the eggs, making them spicy. I loved my new meal! I had grown not only taller, but also able to taste and savour spicy foods.

Later, my father told me that the complete omelette—his original recipe—is omelette with shallot, spring onions, and smashed chilli. But since I wasn't ready when I was four, he changed the recipe to accommodate my young taste buds. As I've said, he started with plain omelette, then added shallots and spring onions when I was a little older, and finally introduced

1 big red chilli and
1 clove of garlic
to make sambal

Omelette
mixture

½ teaspoon
of salt

1 tablespoon of
diced
spring
onion

1 egg

1 diced
shallot

me to the spicy chilli—the complete recipe—when I was ready to savour spicy foods. I believe that the ability to change a recipe for whoever will eat it is the beauty of cooking for loved ones, a beauty and love that my father understood well.

Still, he would not let me cook for myself, not yet. I was not ready.

Time passed, and I matured in many ways. My father used to walk me to school and fetch me at the end of the day, but by age 11, I could walk by myself. I remember, when I was a small child, the school, only two stories high, was a monolith, huge and frightening. Now it seemed small, confining even, though lovely with red clay tiles on the roof and walls in shades of blue.

Palm trees swayed in the breeze as I approached, walking faster. I was excited that day for I was enrolled in a cooking class! I could not wait to learn to do what my father did so well. I imagined his pride when I could cook for myself.

I was one of only a few boys in a classroom full of girls. The girls gathered in cliques, giggling and chattering. I, on the other hand, was very serious about this cooking experience. I listened with rapt attention as my teacher talked about measurements and flavours, tools and recipes. However, even in my cooking class, they hardly ever permitted me to cook! The girls took charge of my group and I was only allowed to wash dishes. Although frustrated, I still paid close attention and I learned a lot.

One day, after I'd been in cooking class for about a month, I came home from school to find my father very tired from his long day of work in the shop. Because he often cooked for me as soon as I got home—I was a growing boy, always hungry—he began to rise from his chair to go and make me my omelette.

"Pa, no," I said. "Sit. Relax. I am old enough to cook my own food now. I can already smell it and taste it in my mouth."

Easing himself back into his seat, my father smiled. "Yes, you are ready now. When you can already smell and taste the food you are about to cook before chopping a single vegetable, you show that you have grown so much love and friendship for that omelette, it is now possible for you to create the best omelette that you would want to eat."

That night my family and I enjoyed the omelette that I cooked for the first time. My father, mother, and even little sister ate every last crumb, savoured every mouthful. And between satisfying my own taste buds and seeing them enjoy my food so heartily, I felt as if I were in heaven.

Unfortunately, growing up, I forgot about my love for that omelette. I began to eat other foods, but they too faded from my memory. Later on, I realized that I should not have forgotten about it. I have learned from my mistake, which is why I share the memory with you now.

We should not forget about our first love in experiencing certain foods. I urge you to please start recollecting good food memories. It doesn't have to be memories from your childhood as it was when I recalled my first omelette. It might be just your good feelings from lunch yesterday or last night during dinner. Keep that good memory. Let it seep through all your senses, and be ready to use all of these memories—from the scent lingering in your nose to the glow in your heart—when you cook for your loved ones. The key is the enjoyment, the fun and heart-warming feelings that you have felt. Remember these feelings and then recreate them in your own food when you cook it for your loved ones.

Back to my story, I grew still older, and not only taller now, but wider—all the crispy junk foods that I still loved had begun to show on my body. By the time I finished college, where I studied Food Technology and IT, I was very fat—120 kg at only 175 cm tall (about 260 lbs, 5 foot 7 inches tall.) I believe that some of my weight came from forgetting to savour and enjoy my food as I had that first omelette. I'd stopped eating with love and stopped infusing my cooking with heart.

After college, I worked in my hometown for about a year, and then I got a job in Jakarta. This led to a job offer in Singapore, a long way from home about five hundred miles across the water and in a different country, even. Five hundred miles may not seem so far, but I had to fly there, and it was a huge distance to my family. I remember my mother being supportive, as she usually was with my ventures, and my father being quiet—as he usually was. He used to go to a quiet place on the third floor of our home to pray for my sister and me. He told my mother that this was the best he could do for us.

I'd intended to stay in Singapore for only a year, save some money, and return to my hometown. It didn't turn out that way...

"Hey, Agus," said one of my colleagues in the elevator of the building where I worked. It was the end of the workday, the workweek, a Friday night. "Some friends and I are going to the cinema tonight. How about you join us?"

"I don't know," I said, sticking my hands deep into my pockets.

Although I'd lost about 30 kg (60 lbs) since moving to Singapore, I was still shy and awkward among other people my age. I worked all the time and had no friends, nor even a desire to make friends. My plan was only to work, work, and work some more and then to move back home.

"Come on! It'll be fun," said my colleague, elbowing me in the ribs.

Shrugging, I agreed. I'd always enjoyed the cinema—my family had gone often when I was growing up. So I went, had a great time, and began to go out with colleagues more and more often. I was introduced to many people and made a lot of new friends. Singapore had begun to feel like home.

One afternoon in 2008, a couple of friends and I were going to see a movie, *Shinjuku Incident,* a Jackie Chan movie we were all looking forward to. We were meeting someone I didn't know, but when she was late, I already didn't like her. In all my 26 years, I'd never been late to the start of a movie!

After a while, we wondered if the girl was going to show up at all. It was hot outside the cinema, about 30 degrees Celsius (85 Fahrenheit), and humid, and when it started to rain, we decided to go inside without the latecomer. I remember feeling very angry with her, even after she did show up—maybe especially then, as she disrupted my enjoyment of the movie when she crept past me to her seat.

"Excuse me. Sorry," she said, nearly upsetting my popcorn as she passed. The nerve of her!

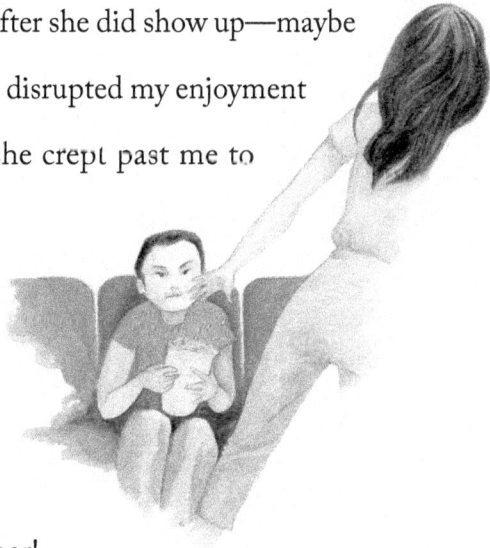

I felt distracted and grew even grumpier the more I thought about this person. I was so upset, I thought perhaps the movie should be called *The Singapore Incident*. I could not get the late girl out of my mind!

After the movie, I was not going to talk to her at all. I did not even look at her. But my friend, Ameh, decided to break the ice—"Aming," she said, using my nickname, "you haven't met this girl before, right? Her name is Frida."

I raised my eyes to glance at her then lowered them again, glowering inside. I did not want to look at this girl who'd ruined my movie experience! From beneath hooded lids, I saw her smile but only politely. She didn't like me either. Although why, I could not imagine. *I* had been on time!

"Hi," we said, then walked away in opposite directions.

It was likely this dark-skinned, admittedly-beautiful girl was thinking, *I hope I don't ever have to see* him *again!*

Certainly, I was thinking that about her!

But again, fate had other plans…

By the following year, I was socializing quite a bit. In 2009, my friends and I decided to take a vacation trip to Yogyakarta, a tourist spot on the coast of Java, replete with Buddhist temples and beaches and fine-dining spots. By this time, I was fairly slender, though I maintained a bit of a tummy. I still loved food.

Because this was a holiday, I decided I should eat as much of the sweet, succulent foods as I could and not worry about my weight.

"Aming is going to grow his belly large again," said my friend, Akie.

"OMG, you just ate tidbits and a heavy breakfast, but you still can eat more?" joked Acim.

Although their teasing was light-hearted and friendly, because I had once been fat, I felt self-conscious. My pale skin reddened and I looked down at my half-empty plate. Like a child, I pushed my remaining food around, sullen. I ate less and less on that trip and grew more and more angry about it.

Finally, one day we were at a food stall that was selling the traditional Gudeg—also known as Green Jack Fruit Sweet Stew—made of sweet, marinated jackfruit and rice cooked in coconut milk and spices. Gudeg is known the world over for its deliciousness. It was sweet and crunchy, flavours and textures I adored. But when I dug into my third serving, the teasing began again.

"It's your third plate. When will you stop?"

"Slow down or you will waste all that hard exercise at the gym, Aming!"

"Do not eat so much. Your jeans are screaming, 'Too tight' already!"

And so on.

Ignoring them, I ordered more and ate with gusto, not caring if I became sick, only wanting them to shut up. Suddenly, I was surprised by a soft voice from across the table.

"It's okay. It's the holiday, right. Enjoy it!" the voice said, and I looked up to see that it was Frida who'd spoken, the same woman who'd been late to the movies, the one I'd vowed never to speak to again!

When I looked at her, Frida gave me the warmest smile any

woman besides my mother had ever given me. The warmth and acceptance emanating from her melted me, made me feel like I had as a child when my father had made me my first omelette to cheer me up.

"Thank you, Ahbee," I said, using Frida's nickname in a gesture of kindness and yes, I believe even then, love.

Although we would eventually marry, at first I was still unsure of my feelings for Frida. We did grow closer after the Yogyakarta trip, seeing each other more and more often. We often went to the cinema together, but sometimes I avoided her too. What I now know to be her passion and enthusiasm for life seemed loud and crass to me at the time. Yet I could not stay away from her either.

One night, after some shopping with a friend, Frida met me in the mall. We didn't have plans to watch any specific movie, so we went to the box office to find any movie that would be starting soon. We found *My Sister's Keeper*. It was a well-known "chick-flick," and I wasn't certain I'd like the movie but I'd already said yes to a movie with Frida, so we bought the tickets.

During the movie, we had so much fun talking. This was the first time I'd met a girl who knew movies, actors, and directors as much as I did, and even somewhat better than I! We were both pleasantly surprised, and our ease together made our friendship grow. Soon we began dating. She loved the way I talked with firm and encouraging words. I loved her sparkling eyes and face full of smiles and fun.

In 2010, I proposed and Frida, my Ahbee, accepted.

At the time, I believed that marriage was a simple thing—just get to a wedding and then live together under one roof. Every weekend go to the cinema and malls. Shop together, eat together, and laugh together. That's it. Nothing complicated.

I said to myself, *I will just have fun with it.* Frida accepted, and we were married in May 2011. Soon after, I learned the hard way that marriage was not as simple a thing as I'd thought it would be.

CHAPTER 2

The Healing Sambal

Our wedding was a simple affair, held in my hometown of Semarang, Indonesia. On a glorious morning of sunshine and warm air tempered by a sweet breeze, we were married in a local church by a Catholic priest. His robe gleamed white and I thought this was a very good omen, a very good start for my married life. Frida also wore white: a stunning, ivory white gown to symbolize her purity and commitment to me.

I waited at the end of the altar in my black suit, nervously running my fingertip along the inside of my collar. Sweat beaded on my forehead. But I could not have been happier to see my beautiful bride come down the aisle toward me, and with her arrival by my side, all nervousness floated away. When the service ended, everyone applauded.

A small group of only family and close friends had attended

the wedding service. Seeing me so happy pleased my parents and sister, and they shone with pride. My heart swelled with pride too, as well as with love for my new bride. As we walked up the aisle at the end of the wedding, holding hands, our palms were warm and our faces glowing.

"Welcome to the family," my mother told Frida, embracing her.

"Welcome to adulthood," said my father, shaking my hand and then deciding to pull me into a big hug. He patted my back. "You are now a man. Now you can really begin to make your life. This is what I have prayed for all these years. Thank you, my son, you have made my dreams for you come true."

After the service, we celebrated with dinner at a restaurant. A larger group of about 200 family and friends attended the party. The meal was traditional Chinese, very good food—love food—that we relished and enjoyed. We ate and sang a nice song led by the MC and had a good time. When we returned to Singapore, we celebrated again at a lunch with friends. My Frida seemed more beautiful and full of grace and passion than I could ever have hoped for. It was a magical time in my life.

Then the wedding with all its glory and the excitement of the celebration were done. Frida and I rented a modest apartment together in the centre of Singapore high up on the 11th floor. We had one bedroom, a small living room, and a simple kitchen only large enough to hold a portable, two-burner gas stove. Our living room held only a two-seater sofa and a medium-sized, rectangle dining table with four chairs. However, Frida had decorated the apartment with love. She hung delicate curtains for our windows and a whiteboard so that we would know each other's busy schedules and could still make time to be together.

We put a TV in front of the sofa, close to the front door. Our apartment, though small and simple, seemed sufficient to us. We didn't even eat at home, but typically met at the end of the workday to eat out. Upon returning to our apartment, we were often so tired, we went directly to bed, to sleep. If we had some energy left, we sat together on the sofa to watch TV. It was a routine that seemed to work for both of us.

So there we were—wedding day, done. Renting a place together, done. Moving into the new place, done. I thought that marriage was as simple as that. But I was wrong. After a while, my question was, "Now what?" But I did not share this worry with Frida. In fact, we hardly talked at all.

On the weekends, we went to malls and shopped. Our apartment was walking distance to some shopping and only about 30 minutes away by bus from the main shopping area on Orchard Road. Unfortunately, we often perused stores and shops in near silence, finding little to say to each other. Although we held hands as we felt we should, it became increasingly clear that we were not happy.

Once, I even asked her, "Beib"—which is our romantic nickname since we started dating—"are you glad you married me?"

"What kind of a question is that?" she said, offended.

I did not ask her again.

Meanwhile, life went on. Since I didn't know what else to do to make Frida and me happy, I spent a lot of money in those early days, using my credit cards to spend more than I had on more than we needed. I bought a new audio system and many gadgets, additions to our life that only served to drive us further apart as we isolated from each other, burying our love in material things that had no substance and provided no real joy.

Still, my intentions were good. I saw that my wife—who had always been the smiley one in our group, loud and boisterous and full of fun—was retreating into herself. She no longer laughed and joked when we were with friends or each other. Her cheerful friends began to shy away from her, which isolated her more and made her even sadder.

I thought that buying her expensive things was the answer, believing that material objects would make her happy again and bring back the light to her eyes. So I bought her many, many expensive gifts—jewellery and more gadgets, clothing, and even food. I tried to impress her by taking her out to more and more expensive restaurants.

I remember one time I presented her with a blue box from Tiffany's. She

opened it and inside lay a beautifully handcrafted necklace. Her face brightened, and I swelled with pride. Finally, I'd done right by my dear wife!

But even as I fastened the clasp around her slender neck, I knew that, in fact, I'd failed again.

"Thank you, Beib," she said, but already her smile had fallen.

The gifts, the gadgets, the restaurants—they were all nothing. To make matters worse, I paid for it all with my credit cards, accruing a debt I could not afford to pay. This made my stomach sour, a discomfort I filled with tidbits and snacks, comfort foods that were not really comforting at all.

One day, Frida tried to advise me that I shouldn't spend so much.

"Beib, we don't need these things," she said. "We cannot afford them either."

My face grew red and my chest swelled, not with pride but with anger. "It's my money. Why do you care?"

I thought that this was what it meant to be a man. I forgot the gentle goodness of my father and had come to believe that spending money was the key to pleasing one's wife and making a good marriage, a good life.

Frida shrugged at my response and the next day, she tried to buy a $20 Couple Cup.

Now I shouted, "Oh, so you can spend money but I cannot?"

Tears rose in her eyes, but she did not cry. Putting the cup down, she turned away from me and my anger. I simmered, rage bubbling just below the surface. How dare she interfere? It was *my* hard-earned money!

Our isolation from others grew with the unease in our relationship. At home, we didn't even bother to sit together on the couch to watch TV. Using tiredness and long workdays as an excuse, we went straight to bed in the evenings. We did not talk, did not eat together, and did not laugh. I have never felt less like a man—as my father had prayed I'd become—than I did during that awful time.

A few days after the cup incident, I remember sending some money home to help out my family.

"It's great that you want to support your family," my wife said. "That's why you should not spend too much on credit cards."

Instead of hearing her concern, all I heard was her nagging me about money yet again. And as usual, I shouted at her—"That's my money. You don't like it when I support my family?"

"That's not what I meant at all!" she replied. Tears welled in her eyes again, and again she did not cry but only begged me, "Why don't you listen to what I said?"

We fought often—the same fights, over and over, always ending the same way. I would yell, and Frida would grow quiet. If she spoke at all, it would hardly be a sentence. Then I'd yell and scold her again. Frida became increasingly withdrawn, and I became more and more angry. Sometimes she'd cry in her sleep.

Instead of meeting that emotion with compassion, I would tell myself, "How childish this girl is! She can only cry, and she does nothing. She can't even explain herself to me!"

Our arguments grew worse. We comforted ourselves with junk food. It was not unusual for us to eat three times the normal serving of fast food and then go directly to bed, to sleep away our anguish and frustration with each other. We ignored each other—Frida, afraid to say anything to me, and I, too frustrated and angry to talk to her.

This went on for some time, until one day when we travelled back to my hometown for a Chinese New Year celebration. We arrived in time for lunch.

For our first meal back home, my mother served us warm steamed rice and marinated pork in sweet soy sauce.

"Your father cooked this for you," Ma said to me. "This is your favourite, right?"

To my wife, Ma said, "Agus loves to eat his father's dishes. So today, we prepared this dish especially for both of you."

"Will you eat with us?" Frida asked graciously.

Shaking her head and smiling, my mother said, "You both eat first and I will continue preparing some other things for tonight's celebration."

Before leaving Frida and me alone, my mother served us another dish, a traditional dish that my mother liked to prepare called Sambal. My mother made Sambal by mixing three to five big red chilli peppers with fermented shrimp paste and a touch of salt and white sugar and then smashing it all together with

MARINATED PORK IN SOY SAUCE

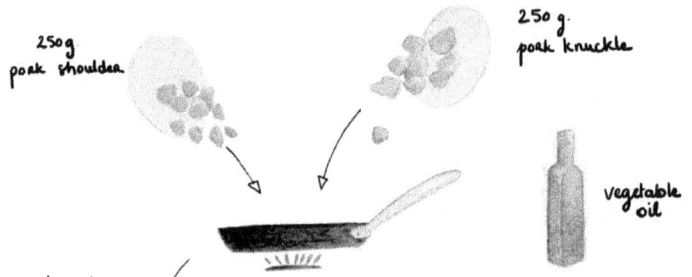

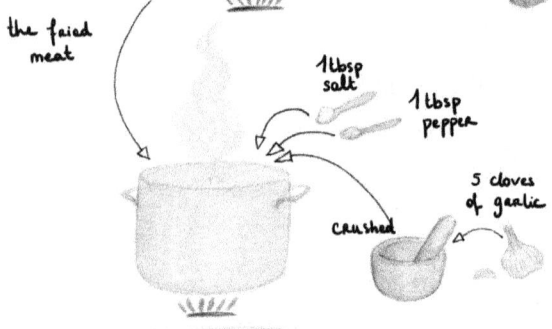

250g pork shoulder

250 g. pork knuckle

vegetable oil

the fried meat

1 tbsp salt

1 tbsp pepper

5 cloves of garlic

crushed

After 1.5 hour

1 cup of sweet soy sauce

Simmer for another 2 - 3 hours

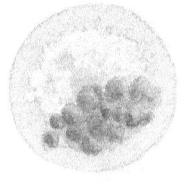

mortar and pestle until it became a smooth puree.

My wife and I enjoyed that lunch so much and so deeply. We felt the warmth of the food not only in our bellies but also in our hearts. Sitting across from Frida at the familiar dining room table in my childhood home, I could see my wife's face brighten again. The smile I'd fallen in love with was back. She ate the marinated pork my father had made with the Sambal that my mom had made and loved it all.

The more Frida ate, the more she smiled, her happiness lighting up her face. The sadness that had darkened her heart disappeared. Even I felt my chest grow lighter, no longer burdened with anger, frustration, and shame.

"This is a great Sambal," Frida said. "It feels like home. It's been a very long time since I last enjoyed this kind of food."

I agreed. It was the first time Frida and I had agreed on anything in quite some time and it felt wonderful. Love and comfort and joy infused my body, comforting me in a way all the junky "comfort" food I'd been eating back in Singapore never could.

My wife and I talked and laughed together again, happily teasing each other the way we used to. It seemed like the Sambal had healed us. I'd forgotten the power of food to do that. During

that lunch, I began to remember.

Later, we celebrated the New Year with my family, beginning

with a walk to the night market. The whole time, my family

never noticed tension between Frida and me. Instead, we all

basked in the warmth of each other's company. On the way

back home from the market, Frida reached for me and took my

hand. I squeezed her hand back as if to say, "I love you, Beib."

Back at my parents' house, we ate a traditional New Year

dinner with sweet and sour Garoupa fish and some barbequed

meat. My grandparents used to eat this same menu since even

before my father got married. Pa also loved to cook braised pork

knuckle or pork belly.

"Gus," he said, "Your

grandma used to cook this

for me when I was young.

It always makes me think

of home."

I nodded. It felt like

home to me, too. That

homey feeling—the love, the

warmth, the sweet comfort—was something that no trinkets or gadgets had done for our apartment in Singapore.

My mother served us more Sambal with the braised pork my father made, also following tradition. Ma's own mother had always made Sambal to go with braised pork because the pork was so sweet. The spicy flavours of the Sambal made a delicious counterpoint to that sweetness, warming all of my insides, from the surface of my tongue to the depth of my heart.

Frida and I touched fingers under the table. We were whole again. And during that celebration, all the family in my hometown enjoyed our company without ever finding out how much we'd been fighting lately, all thanks to my mother's Sambal and my father's marinated pork.

Because the trip home was such a success, I believed my family didn't know anything about Frida and my recent marital troubles. However, perhaps they did realize we were struggling because just before Frida and I headed to the airport, my mother made us lunch again, and over lunch, she asked me, "Do you still cook?"

I raised my eyebrows in shock. I hadn't expected that question at all. Why would she suspect that I wasn't cooking anymore?

Did she notice that I was unhappy? Or that Frida was? Was I growing fat again? I couldn't make sense of it. I'd thought Frida and I had fooled everyone, and yet here was my mother, staring hard at me as if she knew everything—even more than I'd realized myself.

"Well, with my new job and Frida's work too, we are very busy. Not much time for cooking," I said, turning my eyes downward in shame.

"I understand that you are busy with your work, but I hope that you still remember how cooking can bring you closer to your loved ones," said my father. "Like I used to cook for you."

I felt the anger and frustration that had plagued me for months rising in me again. I was determined to keep the secret of my unhappiness, even from those who loved me most. "Okay. Got it. But we *are* busy. Still no time to cook."

My parents shrugged and didn't question me any further. But I could see the worry in their eyes.

Although at the time I could not see how secrecy and shame were hurting me and my marriage, the experience of my holiday back home with my parents eventually taught me a valuable lesson—that we should not "excuse" ourselves with lies and cover-ups. Making an excuse—such as being too busy to cook—is easy to do, but those excuses will lead us to what I call a "relationship black hole." Excuses ruin our chances to have good relationships. That was what happened to me.

The excuse I made up to hide my feelings from my parents became a lie I told myself as well. I repeated the same excuse in my head over and over again after that trip, meanwhile doing nothing to work on my relationship with Frida. Instead, I fell back on old habits and routines, the routines of a daily job keeping me too busy to fight for my marriage, and the routine of fighting over small matters with my wife keeping me too busy to look at my part in the deterioration of our relationship.

We truly were very busy working, however. My wife even took on a part-time job in addition to her full-time job during this time. Normally, she'd meet me for dinner at around seven, then we'd take the bus home together, but on days when she worked at her other job as well, she didn't come home until ten or eleven at night. These were hard times for Frida and me.

One Saturday while Frida was at work, I turned on a cooking show. Although I wasn't cooking at home and Frida didn't cook either, we liked to watch cooking shows. Sometimes it was just

to spend some time together between work and bed. When
I watched alone, I thought it was only that I didn't have to
concentrate on the show but could do other things at the same
time. But upon reflection, I believe I was drawn to cooking
shows because my heart was still that of a cook.

The chef on the show that day was cooking steak in front of a
bunch of kids. The kids looked happy and it brought me back to
when I was a child and my father would cook for me. Although
I hadn't thought of that time in my life for a long while, I was
transported back to the warmth and aromas of my childhood
home whenever my father stood at the stove. I remembered the
sweetness of his love for me and how he expressed it through
his cooking. At the same time, I recalled his words to me when
Frida and I had been home for New Year—when he'd told me
never to be too busy to cook for my loved one.

After the show ended, I went straight to the supermarket and bought enough ingredients to cook steak, fried rice, and pasta for the next two days. I imagined how fancy my food would be and all the compliments my wife would give me when she tasted it.

When Frida came home that night, she kicked off her tight shoes and sank into the couch, exhausted. "Beib, I am so tired. I dread going out again. I just want to sit here until bedtime!"

Smiling with pride, I said, "Don't worry, we don't have to go out tonight. I will cook something for dinner. You just wait and see."

Frida smiled that big smile that I'd fallen in love with. In my short pants and tee shirt—looking a lot like my father used to when he'd cooked for me—I went to our small kitchen area with its two-burner stove top and prepared our meal. Although

I used some of what I'd seen on the cooking show, I hadn't watched it that closely. Using my imagination, I used a lot of seasoning. I mixed soy sauce, mushrooms, and beef stock for a sauce. The addition of soy sauce was my own invention and I did it to elevate what should have been simple food into something more elaborate—a fusion dish, I thought. The whole while I cooked, I pictured myself as a chef, creating recipes that people waited in line to taste. My wife was a lucky woman to have me in the kitchen!

However, I was so busy fantasizing about my food creation, I made several mistakes. For one thing, the meat was terribly overcooked. But I didn't know that until later because I didn't even bother to taste my cooking before serving it to Frida and myself. And then, when we began to eat, I focused more on gulping down my own portion than on watching Frida's reaction.

My steak was too salty and very tough. No matter, I told myself. "This is what fusion food is supposed to taste like."

We didn't talk during the meal but as soon as we were done I asked with a broad smile, "How was it?"

I expected high praise for my fancy, fusion creation.

Instead, Frida said, "It's okay, but tough to chew."

The nerve of her! I was so angry inside, even though I'd had trouble chewing the same meat. I knew it was too salty and tough, but I wouldn't admit defeat. Instead, I thought, "I will make even fancier food tomorrow."

The next night, I again focused more on my fantasies of being a great chef and creating amazing food than I did on actually cooking something delicious. Again, I didn't watch for Frida's reaction as she ate my "restaurant quality" meal of fried rice with salty soy sauce and dried fish.

Again, when I asked her how she liked it, she said only, "It tastes okay."

Still unhappy with Frida's response to my cooking, I cooked again for dinner the next night—pasta, also with salty soy sauce and some minced meat. During dinner, my wife didn't say anything and I didn't bother to ask, quickly finishing my own food.

I continued on like this for months, cooking and failing to get the praise I believed I so richly deserved. Perhaps somewhere inside I knew that my food wasn't right, the way I was cooking wasn't the right way. But I covered those thoughts with more prideful ones—"She doesn't know how lucky she is, having someone to cook great meals for her."

Then one day, my wife and I were watching a cooking show together before bed. "My food is better than that," I said. "You've tried it. I'm right, aren't I?"

Frida shrugged. "Your food tastes okay," she said, "but everything tastes the same. Pasta, steak, fried rice, seafood stir fry, veggie stir fry, and so on. It is all very salty with soy sauce and not much else to season it. But that's fine. I suppose every person has their signature taste in their food."

What? She did not love my food? It was too salty? I was furious.

"So you insult me. Okay, no more cooking. You will never see me cooking again. You would never understand my food anyway."

"You don't listen carefully," said my wife, imploring me with tear-filled eyes to please understand her. "I didn't say I don't like your cooking. I said perhaps every person has their signature taste in their food and that's fine."

But "fine" wasn't good enough for me. "Great" or "superb" maybe, but just "fine"? I simmered with rage and frustration. Inside I knew she was right, but those feelings were buried deep, hidden under dark thoughts and anger.

"I don't care," I said, folding my arms and narrowing my eyes. "You insulted my food."

After that, our fighting grew worse. I thought Frida didn't support or understand me. I scolded her frequently. Meanwhile, she grew more and more quiet, as was her way. I began to give up on us in my heart and even mentioned divorce. She resumed crying in her sleep.

I remembered before Frida and I were married when a friend had asked me, "What do you like about Frida that makes you want her for your future wife?"

I answered, "I like that she's simple and naive and most of

the time says something wrong in a funny way, and with that, I can always laugh with her."

"What if someday things changed?" my friend had asked me at the time.

I'd thought it was a ridiculous question and had only laughed. But after months of fighting with my wife, I began to see what my friend had meant. The things that had made me fall in love with Frida had become the things that I hated the most about her.

I used to laugh when she said something wrong just because she didn't understand things, but after we got married it made me furious. I also used to laugh when she asked about something that even a child should know, but after we got married, I hated it because I thought these were stupid questions. And whereas before, I'd loved the way she spoke simply about everything, yet after we married, I hated it because I believed that only stupid people thought so simply. I preferred detailed explanations and I rarely got that from my wife. Most of the time, I didn't understand what she was thinking.

This experience taught me a very valuable lesson. We should never make assumptions about our loved ones. We especially should never assume what he or she would want to eat.

I thought that my food was great and yet never even tasted it when I cooked. That is not how one cooks for a loved one. I might as well have served my food to a pet, not a human being with complicated feelings and taste buds.

At this point, you may remember how I'd said in the previous chapter that we should preserve our good memories of food and recreate it in our cooking. But as you can see, I didn't do that and even worse, I made high assumptions about my food and about what my wife wanted to eat. I now believe, and hopefully you too can see, that such hubris brought my relationship to an even darker place.

Our fighting grew worse. Although I could not imagine living without Frida, I also could not take the pain of constantly struggling and bickering. We had become quite cruel to each other, hardly speaking, and when we did, it was to insult each other. I came very close to calling our parents and telling them that we were getting a divorce. This would have shocked them, as Frida and I had kept our struggles secret, and neither our families nor our friends knew how close we were to ending the marriage. Keeping this darkness inside made me a different person, very angry all the time.

Then, one Sunday, about a year after our wedding, a small miracle occurred. I remember it was a rainy afternoon, the water a pleasant patter on the roof, sliding over the windows like God's tears. Frida and I woke from an afternoon nap and settled on the couch to watch a cooking show together—despite the trouble in our marriage, we still watched cooking shows and went to the cinema together.

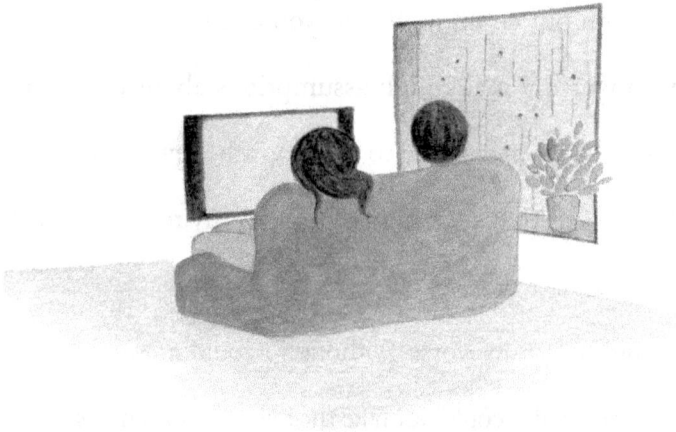

The show that day was about cooking traditional Indonesian food. It was almost a shock to hear my wife's voice say softly— without malice or criticism, as I'd grown used to hearing in her tone—"That Sambal looks nice. I want to eat it like that with warm steamed rice. It would taste like heaven. Just like your mother's Sambal and your father's marinated pork worked great together."

This revelation struck me, strumming the chords of my heart. *Why didn't I think of that?* I thought to myself. *All this while, I did everything on my own. I closed my life from my wife. Actually, now I believe that cooking for her can still do good for our relationship.*

Almost as if she'd heard my private thoughts, my wife suddenly said, "I feel starving now after watching that show."

"What do you want to eat? Can I cook it for you?" I replied.

Those are the questions that I should have asked a long time ago. *What do you want to eat?*—and—*Can I cook it for you?*

Not assume what she wanted to eat. *Talk* to her. *Share* with her.

And my wife, who usually kept her thoughts and feelings to herself, said simply, "I want to eat something with Sambal."

Since my wife is a woman of few words, I needed to translate her desire into something more detailed. So I took a while to think about it carefully. Because I didn't want to be disappointed cooking fancy stuff that she would not like, I thought I should try simple cooking instead. The thing that popped into my head was my father's omelette from my childhood. The one he'd infused with his love for me.

I remembered how my father mixed his omelette with chilli. I decided I would cook an omelette, and as my wife had requested, I would make Sambal, just like my mom did, and serve it with nice steamed rice. To be certain I would please her, I then told my wife about my plan.

"That's actually a super idea," she said. With a new lightness to my step, I hurried to the nearest supermarket and bought all the ingredients.

When I returned, I started cooking right away, beginning with steaming rice in the rice cooker. Then I cooked the omelette just like my father had cooked it, but, of course, I doubled the ingredients because it was meant for both Frida and me. I used two chicken eggs, two diced shallots, and about one stem of a spring onion. I seasoned it with a bit of salt to taste. Then I fried it in a pan with about five tablespoons of oil.

While I fried the omelette, the nice smell started to fill our small apartment. The aroma brought me back to the time I'd cooked my first omelette for my mother and father. My eyes glistened as the emotions I'd felt back then flooded my heart and mind... how

I'd felt so fulfilled when I first cooked for my parents... how I felt when I tasted my first own omelette with steamed rice. My heart warmed, just as it had back in my childhood.

So I kept those memories active while I cooked that omelette for my wife. I did not imagine her praising my food. I simply tried my best to make something tasty and soulful for my wife, something that would make her feel the way I had when my father used to cook specially for me. I wanted Frida to feel as though she were the most important woman in the world to me. I wanted her to taste the depth of my love for her in my cooking.

Since there was no salty soy sauce in my father's recipe, I didn't put it in Frida's omelette, unlike all the other food that I'd cooked for my wife previously. After the omelette was cooked, I started making my Sambal.

I cut five small red chillies, three big red chillies, and one clove of garlic with scissors. Then I fried the chillies and the garlic together with the fermented shrimp paste as my mom had done. At that time, I didn't have a mortar and pestle, so I transferred all the ingredients from the frying pan into a small bowl and mashed it with the back of a spoon. My Sambal was finally completed, with a bit of rough chilli pieces in it. This

SAMBAL
Recipe

Cut into small pieces

3x
big red chilli

5x
small red chilli

1x
clove of garlic

Fry with

1 tbsp of
fermented shrimp
paste

1 tbsp
of
vegetable
oil

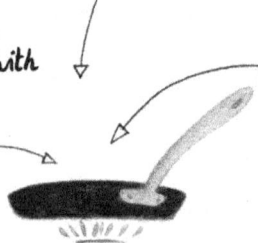

Transfer all
and
crush it
with dining spoon

time I tasted everything before I served it.

My wife and I ate together, and that night, Sambal again healed our wounds, just as it had the previous New Year in my hometown. We told each other funny stories; for example, I told her about when we'd first met at the cinema, and how I'd gone on to call *Shinjuku Incident* the "*Singapore Incident*." Frida laughed that boisterous laugh from when we were first together. She reached out and touched my fingertips with hers. We were one again.

This reminded me of another story, which I shared with Frida. I told her how my friend Akie had told me, "Aming, wait until you meet this girl. She has the biggest laugh you'll ever hear."

My wife even opened up to me for the first time since we'd been married. She explained why she was so worried about my credit card spending and debt. It seemed her friends had told her to be wary of that.

We left the plates on the table and the pans unwashed in the kitchen, retiring to the bedroom to continue our talk. It was so lovely to sit in the warmth of our humble abode, snuggled under the covers while the rain continued on outside. For the first time in a year, we were happy, in our own world. Squeezing my hand, Frida told me how much she loved our friendship when we were more open to each other and encouraged each other. That friendship had seemed to be gone but now it was back, stronger than ever.

"We actually have many chances to have a nice life," I said to her. "But I was so stupid that I didn't see that. Please forgive me for how hard I was on you."

My wife smiled, happy and full of joy again to hear me say that. "I think we should do this more often," she said. "Your food tonight didn't taste the same as your previous dishes."

Bowing my head, I humbly replied, "Thank you."

The bright, shining smile on my wife's face made me remember how I used to smile whenever I ate my father's omelette and how my parents had glowed when they'd eaten my omelette all those years ago.

That night was really a turning point in our marriage. I kept those good memories in my heart whenever I cooked for my wife after that, recreating the love and emotion in my cooking. I asked her the right questions and I never assumed I already knew what she was going to say or feel. And eventually, this stopped the apocalypse from descending on our marriage.

That night I also understood that this was just a start. But now I was equipped with better tools to improve my relationship. I knew that it wouldn't always be a smooth journey, but I only had to keep trying and not give up on us as I had before… not let the darkness into my heart but keep my soul full of love and friendship.

And I was right. After that night, I continued to cook for my wife based on what she wanted and the good memories and feelings we'd shared. Our relationship thrived. We were affectionate and respectful of each other. Though we sometimes argued—as all couples do—we were not cruel to each other as we had been.

Sadly, after just a few weeks of enjoying our newly improved relationship, life dragged us down again… The credit card bills piled up because I hadn't listened to my wife's early warnings, the rented apartment contract was almost over and the owner

increased the fee, and to make matters worse, my father grew ill.

This made me worry all the time, especially whenever I received

text messages from my hometown. I wondered how Frida and

I would endure such challenges to our married life.

CHAPTER 3

The Homey Tomato Soup

LIFE will always come at us, sometimes softly—an angel's wing, beating against our cheeks, or a warm meal tucked away in our bellies… sometimes hard—creditors rapping at the door. And we will always reap what we sow. Thus, all my overspending with credit cards caught up with me.

I'd never told my wife how much I'd spent, nor did I know how I would pay these huge bills. There Frida and I were, growing closer day by day, and still, I kept these secrets from her. I was too proud, and I believed I could handle my debts on my own. No need to worry her, no need to drive a wedge between us,

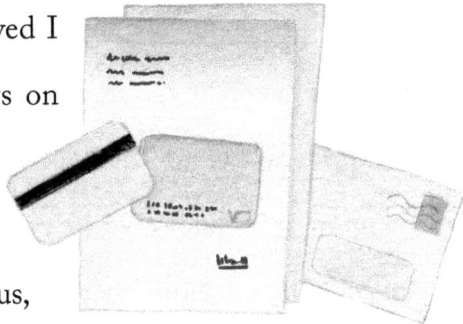

53

I thought. And then, one day, we received a letter about the rent. It was being raised by 30 percent.

My wife paced our small living room, winding a strand of hair around her finger and tugging at it in her distress. "Do you think we can afford it?" she said. "How much do you pay for your credit cards each month? Because it seems that every month, the money is gone before we've paid all our bills."

As usual, when my wife asked me about money, I felt anger uncoiling like a snake inside me. But although I wanted to lash out at Frida, something came over me, and I only said, "Why don't we eat lunch first. What do you want to eat? Can I cook it for you?"

Suddenly the mood changed. Whereas before we'd been spun up with emotion, now we were calm. My wife stopped pacing to think about what she would like to eat. My head filled with ideas of how I could provide the best food for my wife and that centred my mind on love, care, and tenderness—not bitterness, fear, and pride, as before. This experience taught me that even the intention to cook for my wife could give us a helpful bit of time to cool off before discussing sensitive issues.

After a few moments, my wife smiled and said, "Something

simple will do. But I miss home and would love some Indonesian food."

I remembered that we had just bought some Indonesian sweet soy sauce, so I decided to cook a simple omelette just as my father had for me, with steamed rice and that same sweet sauce. Sitting at our modest table, we ate and enjoyed each other's company.

When we were through, Frida looked at me with soft eyes and I knew it was time to be honest with her about my debt. So I told her the truth with a soft and humble voice. Meeting my gentler self with love, she did not berate me, as I'd feared she would. Rather, we worked together on figuring out how we might resolve our money problems.

"I have promised your family that we will continue to live in Singapore. And living in this tiny, rented apartment is not really suitable for building a family of our own, as we would like to do. Also, if we continue to pay rent, and a higher rent at that, we will just be burning our money. Wouldn't it be better to buy an apartment?"

My wife twisted her hair around her finger again in worry but remained calmly seated as she thought and then said, "But we don't have the money for a down payment. And you also have a great deal of responsibility to help your family lately, since your father has frequently fallen ill."

My head dipped as I forced myself not to cry. But tears rose in my eyes anyway when I thought about the tremendous stress I was under, worrying about my family. My mother often texted me with news that used to be largely good news, but recently it had been mostly bad.

I rose from my seat and cleared the lunch dishes. As I rinsed them in the sink, I tried to come up with a plan for Frida and me to have the family we dreamed of and still pay all our bills. With a sigh, I realized that I could not solve this alone. I returned to the table.

"I'm sorry that you must worry about money like this. I thought I could handle our finances on my own. But I realize now that I can't, and I'm ready to show you my credit card bills now."

My wife reached out and touched my shoulder to show her support as I began to walk away to get the bills. Standing still for a moment, I patted her hand as if I knew it would all be all right now.

"Thank you for sharing this with me," Frida said. "Now that I know about it, I can be more prepared and can endure it together with you. That's the point of being married, right?"

When she said that, my heart melted and tears rose in my eyes again. I now understood how good, simple food could open the heart. My wife's words were simple but powerful. I felt encouraged and less stressed than I had in some time.

✐

One warm day in 2012, close to the Chinese New Year, I received good news from my mother. My father was feeling better than he had in some time. When Frida and I arrived, and I saw that my father was indeed feeling well, I felt my shoulders loosen and my burdens lift.

I felt even better after seeing my sister, whom I hadn't seen in some time. Her fair skin glowed when she introduced me to her boyfriend, who smiled much as my father always had. I liked the young man immediately and was glad to find my sister was serious about him. We all crammed together happily in my parents' house, laughing and teasing, eating and singing—enjoying the New Year celebration and each other's company.

Shortly after the new year, I took my parents aside and told them about our hope to buy our own apartment—nothing fancy, but one in good condition and big enough for us to start a family. My mouth dry and hands sweaty, I looked my father in the eyes as I told him the truth, that we didn't have enough money for a down payment. We had fought bitterly about money in the past, so this admission from me was especially hard to make.

Taking my hands in his, my father said something I did not expect. "We all support your decision. Don't worry about the money. We'll get it for you."

Relief flooded my senses and this time tears did slide down

my cheeks, tears of joy and gratitude. "I will repay you, every cent," I said.

My father only smiled as he always did, trusting me—as he always did.

True to their word, my parents secured a bank loan and let me know just before it was time for me to fly back to Singapore that the loan had been approved and was processing. In a few short weeks, Frida and I would have the money for our down payment! With this good news warming our hearts, we got on a plane. Meanwhile, my sister and her boyfriend took off by car back to Surabaya.

"Everything is settled," I said to my wife on the plane. She smiled and kissed me lightly on the cheek.

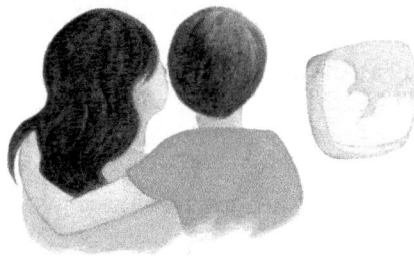

"I knew it would be," she said.

But it wasn't. Instead, more problems came knocking on our door.

We'd just gotten back home to Singapore and were preparing for sleep when my mother called to tell me that my sister and her boyfriend had been in an accident. Their car had been hit by a truck and both of them had been severely injured. My sister's boyfriend went back home to be cared for by his parents and to receive treatment for a dislocated hip. Meanwhile, my sister had to move in with my parents so that my mother could care for her.

My sister had several broken bones and other injuries. She was in such bad shape, she could not even use the toilet by herself for several months. My mother had to do everything for her. Of course, I worried that this would leave my mother too strained to care enough for my father, whose health was not as good as he'd led us to believe during New Year, with his gentle smiles and stoic attitude.

Fearful for my family, I called home one day and my mother told me, "Your father said not to worry, just keep going. We believe that you will find the best apartment for your family. Your father also said, 'Don't stop cooking for your wife. I heard great things from your wife about your cooking when both of you visited us last Chinese New Year.'"

This cheered me up some, and, feeling better—and also to honour my parents—Frida and I began searching for an apartment to buy. Before long, we found one that we loved.

It was about 45 minutes outside the city by train and was smallish, but had two bedrooms, a living room with a dining area, and a kitchen. Plenty large enough for us to start a family. It did need some work on the second bedroom and the kitchen but it had great potential.

We decided to buy it, although my wife still worried, as was her way—"Do you think it's okay? We could use the money to help your family instead."

Pulling her into a close embrace, I said, "It's okay! I still have some savings with which to help them. The best way to help right now will be to cheer them up by finding the best apartment."

I was right. A few weeks later, when the purchase of our new apartment was settled and a contractor had been hired to make the necessary repairs, I called home to let them know.

"That's wonderful!" said my mother.

"We're very proud, Gus, proud and happy for you and Frida," my father added.

"I can't wait to visit!" exclaimed my sister.

But again, the happiness was short-lived, for just a few days later, my mother messaged me with terrible news.

"Gus, your father fell getting out of bed. He hurt his elbow very badly and will need surgery."

I flew down the next afternoon to be with my family. My father was, as usual, smiling and stoic, trying not to make a big deal over his condition. But seeing him in that bed waiting for surgery scared me. His skin was ashen, his body frail. This was not the strong, full-bodied man who had stood in the kitchen chopping green onions and frying me an omelette... Physically, that man was gone, except for his smile and his eyes, which still shone with the same love for his family as ever.

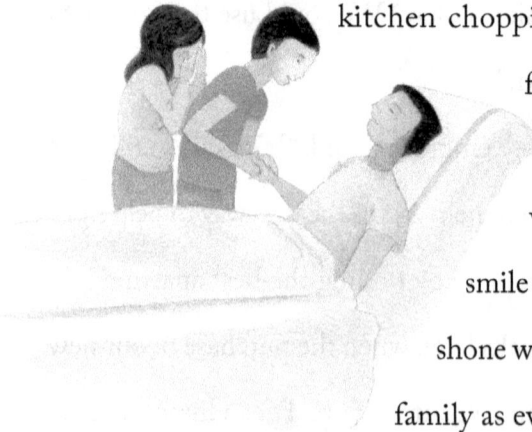

The surgery was a wretched three hours long. My mother cried softly and there was nothing I could do to console her. Finally, the surgeon emerged to tell us that my father was going to be fine. However, I noticed that he looked away from our faces as if he was more worried than he wanted us to be. I wondered what he wasn't telling us but could do nothing about it.

My heart ached to see the room my father was placed in, a stifling hot room shared with three others. Dusty windowsills and even spider webs in the corners. But it was the best I could afford. Frida's warning ran through my head in a continuous loop as I worried about the apartment. Could we afford it? Should we hold on to the money in case my family needed it?

While my father slept, I held my mother's hand. I told her honestly, "I couldn't keep my promise to Pa that I would continue cooking for Frida. These last few months have been so horrible. Hopefully Pa and Ratna will get better soon and everything will be back to normal. Then I will cook again. In the new apartment, I will cook, just as I promised."

Squeezing my hand, my mother said, "It's all right. Remember—as your father always showed you—the cooking itself is important, but it is not everything. What is most important is to keep the *spirit* of making good food for your loved one in your heart, even when you are not cooking. You must remember to put her first. Whether it is by cooking food she loves or making her a simple cup of tea or coffee, it does not matter. What matters is that your ego becomes smaller as you care for your wife."

I sat quietly, thinking over what my mother had said while waiting for my father to return to us.

He did wake up, but he looked tired. His skin was still ashen and he soon fell back to sleep. That night, his condition worsened. He got an infection and a terrible fever. Although I wanted to stay with my family, I needed to return to Singapore to work because my salary would help pay the hospital bills, not to mention still paying for my own credit card debt. My whole body sagged with the weight of my sorrow as I said good-bye.

"It will be fine," my mother said.

But instead, my father grew worse and worse. And in June of 2012, my mother called to tell me that my father had passed away. My heart broke upon hearing the news. I wanted to howl out loud but remained quiet as I held my wife close. She cried the tears that I could not for fear that once I started crying, I might not stop.

We went back to Semarang for my father's funeral, a Buddhist ceremony full of song and prayer meant to lead my father into his next life. With a heavy heart, I carried the picture of my father to the cremation area. And as the eldest son, it was my job to press the button on the incinerator. I finally cried for this man I had loved so dearly and who had loved me even more.

The hardest part of that time was when, just before the funeral, my mother had showed me what was in the cupboard where my father kept money from his shop. There were two boxes, one labelled with my sister's name and one with mine. I remembered how my father had always said not to worry about money, that he would save money from the shop for us. And I remembered that he had opened his shop every morning when we were young, even if business was slow.

But there was no money in the boxes. My father had never earned enough to put any money aside. Yet when we were small, he'd denied us nothing, be it toys or food or going to the cinema. He'd given us all that he had. Yet I'd always wanted more, always asked for more.

That night at the funeral, I cried in front of my father's photo, asking for his forgiveness for my selfishness. The prayer leader comforted me, telling me that it was all right and that my father was moving on to a new and better life, without pain or money troubles.

After the funeral, I thought about how I had not cooked for my father since that first omelette when I was a schoolchild. I remembered that and I knew what he would have wanted me to do. He would have wanted me to cook for my loved ones as he had for me. That night, I promised in my heart to care for my wife, and to keep my father's spirit alive through cooking for her as I'd told him that I would. I vowed to keep the legacy of my father alive by building the life and family he would have wanted me to have.

And so, my wife and I moved into our new apartment two months later. Because my father had left me with the spirit of cooking, the first thing I did was set up my new kitchen with a new knife set, stainless steel pots, and a ceramic frying pan. But it wasn't enough. Shortly after we moved in, I noticed my wife was doing that pacing she always did when she was feeling uneasy. Looking closer, I saw that her smile was gone, her face crumpled with sadness.

"What's wrong?" I asked, approaching and embracing her.

Laying her head against my shoulder she said, "I don't know, exactly. It just feels somehow wrong here, even though it's better than our rented apartment. It doesn't feel like home."

I agreed. Although we'd renovated the apartment before moving in and I'd tidied up the kitchen, the rest of the apartment lacked hominess. But instead of worrying more about it in that moment, we snuggled together in bed to watch a cooking show, something that always cheered us up. This time it wasn't the show that inspired me; it was a commercial, showing some rice and homemade soup.

I remembered my father telling me how, before he was married, my grandmother had made the family her own special chicken soup with dried squid. My father had told me how much that soup made him feel loved and accepted and at home. I knew then just what to do.

"It's lunch time," I said, sitting up. "What do you want to eat? I think it's time I do my first cooking in this new place. I think soup will make us warmer, not only in our tummies but also in our hearts."

Frida thought for a moment and then said, "The tomato soup in that TV commercial looked nice."

I was surprised and a little resistant at first. I'd thought that I could simply cook chicken soup, the way my grandmother had. But as I swung my legs out of the bed, I thought, "My father's legacy is that I should cook anything that my wife wants to eat."

Nodding and smiling at Frida, I said, "Okay, I'll cook it for you. I need to go to the supermarket for ingredients."

Joining me by the front door to put on her own shoes as I put on mine, Frida told me, "And while you're food shopping, I'll look for some things that will spruce up our place—maybe curtains and a tablecloth. Some small decorations. I don't know, but something nice to make this apartment look more like home."

And so we set out with warmth already in our hearts.

On my way to the supermarket, I passed through an electronics store and saw something that made me stop and think. Chef Jamie Oliver was on TV, broadcasting from Italy, where he showed how the people there make sauce and soup from scratch, using fresh tomatoes and ingredients rather than using canned tomatoes. My stomach growled just to think of this simple way of cooking.

Watching that video, I realized if we compare the meals served in many of the kitchens today to the meals served about 50 years ago, there is one very big difference. Nearly every meal served in

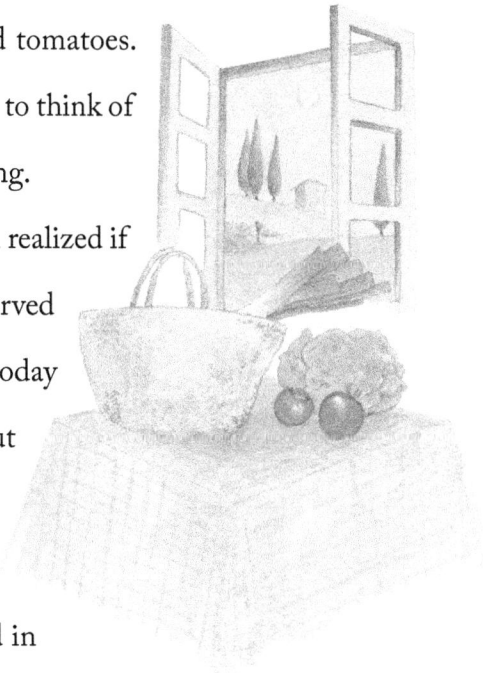

today's world has at least one dish that has come from a box, bag, or pouch. All of this easy-access food has taken a deeper toll on society than you might imagine...

A toll on our health...

A toll on our waistlines...

A toll on our ability to make the simplest items on our own...

A toll on the time we spend with our families...

A toll on the next generation, when we fail to teach them the arts—such as cooking from scratch—which vanish as our parents pass away...

Cooking from scratch is actually an analogy for today's society. Those who take the road less travelled are considered eccentric, throwbacks to a faraway time. People feel that we make unnecessary work for ourselves and that our lives would be vastly improved by tossing an instant food into the grocery cart instead of taking a couple of hours to mix the fresh ingredients. But by cooking from scratch, we put more valuable effort into making sure that our loved ones will enjoy the best food that we can offer to them. Furthermore, when we cook from fresh ingredients, we don't need to worry about potentially harmful food additives.

So I decided to create the tomato soup from fresh tomatoes, carrots, and onions, just as I'd seen in the video I'd watched earlier.

When I got to the supermarket, I headed straight for the vegetable aisle. I noticed there were two different areas for vegetables—organic vegetables in one spot and what appeared to be "normal" vegetables in the other area. Initially, I looked at the prices and decided to take the cheaper ones, the non-organic. But then I paused. I thought about it again and realized that since I only cook for two of us, I didn't need to buy the cheaper vegetables that came in big bags. I could afford to get the organic ones, and when I compared the "normal" and the organic vegetables, I found that the colour and the plumpness of the vegetables were totally different. It seemed as if the farmer who processed the organic vegetables did a lot more careful work because the organic vegetables seemed almost hand-chosen to be more appealing for my cooking.

Of course, after getting my vegetables, I needed to get some other ingredients. With my wife's feelings and health

at the forefront of my mind, I chose the next ingredients even more carefully. I chose the best beef that I could find and afford and also some fresh oregano.

Recently, I talked to an organic food expert and found out that organic produce is grown without the use of pesticides, synthetic fertilizers, sewage sludge, genetically modified organisms, or ionizing radiation. These facts have made me continue to choose organic produce and to feel even better about it. What if I picked just any ingredients and, in the end, caused my wife to become sick? Then I'd have to pay for doctors and even worse, she wouldn't dare touch my food again because of the trauma! When we cook for someone, their life is in our hands. So we'd better do our best.

I left the supermarket feeling light in my heart. My wife met me outside and we walked home together, hand in hand, talking and laughing. While I made the soup, she unloaded her purchases—some hand towels and a soap dispenser, a bright blue wall clock, little things that made our apartment look homier.

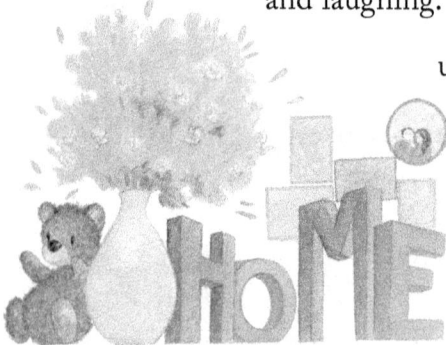

The smell of my carefully chosen ingredients filled the air as I cooked. Inhaling deeply, I smiled. *Home.*

I started my soup by boiling five big ripe red tomatoes with ¼ cup of water in the stainless steel pot that I'd bought when we moved in to our new place. Once boiled, I strained the softened tomatoes to puree them.

Then I boiled my diced beef, one diced carrot, and one diced onion for about 30 minutes. After that, I put in my tomato puree. I added some salt and pepper to taste and a sprig of fresh oregano. Recalling how much my wife loved hot and spicy food, I also added one teaspoon of chilli powder to heat things up.

To make my soup more filling, I put in one handful of shell macaroni. Then I let the whole thing simmer for another 10 to 15 minutes, until the macaroni and beef were soft.

My wife came to the table when I called, and I served the soup. As I ladled some into her bowl, I bowed my head slightly and said, almost like a prayer, "I hope you like it. Let's enjoy it together."

We sipped the soup slowly from our spoons, enjoying the taste. Sometimes we closed our eyes to feel the hot soup flowing through our mouths to our tummies and the warmth flowing to

TOMATO SOUP

Boil

5 big tomatoes

with ¼ cup of water

Puree the softened tomatoes

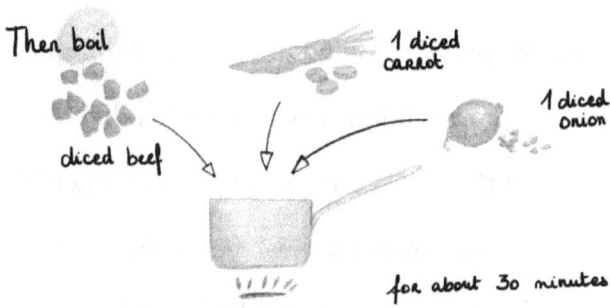

Then boil

diced beef

1 diced carrot

1 diced onion

for about 30 minutes

Add the tomato puree, salt and pepper to taste and a sprig of fresh oregano

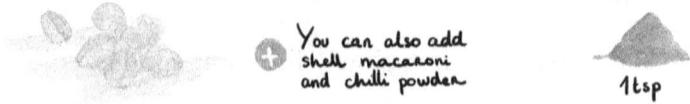

You can also add shell macaroni and chilli powder

1 tsp

our hearts. We finally felt welcome in our new place. All things felt friendlier. A breeze coming through the big window in the living room blew softly upon us.

For the first time, I felt the good feelings that come from being at home and even from growing up. After the soup was gone, Frida and I closed our eyes for a while and inhaled deeply. This was our home, sweet home.

By taking what I'd seen my father do in my youth and translating it into my own adult home, I felt the power of cooking reinforced in me. I learned that to be successful at cooking for our loved ones we must surrender to the process, be it choosing the ingredients, cooking them, or serving our food. We must not only choose the best ingredients, but also the best utensils and other cooking implements, as poor-quality pots will result in bad-tasting food as surely as anything else—and may be detrimental to our health as well, as residue from cheaper metals may get into our food and thus, our bodies.

There's an old Chinese saying I once heard my aunts telling some of the women in my family:

"To fill your husband's heart with you, first you have to fill his stomach with the food that you cook, so that he will always come back home to you."

After making my tomato soup that day, I realized the truth of that saying. I understood what an intimate act eating is, because the food we ingest becomes part of us. And when I smelled the aroma of my soup simmering in the pot, I understood how important even the smell of cooking food could be. It reminds us of other meals. It makes us feel at home. It brings love to our hearts…

And it creates new memories. Just as I will always remember the aroma of my father's omelette whenever I visit my childhood home, I will always remember the scent of my tomato soup in my own home.

CHAPTER 4

The Scrambled Egg Remedy

NEW apartment, new life.

Our apartment felt like home, with a new sofa and dining room table given to us by my in-laws, knick-knacks and other decorative items provided by Frida, and often the aroma of good food wafting out of my kitchen. I'd gotten a new job with higher pay and was able to start paying off my credit card debt. Frida had quit her part-time job and was home with me more. My mother had taken over my father's shop and was adjusting well to life without him. My sister and her boyfriend were planning their wedding... Life was very good.

But it was not perfect. Life seldom is.

One evening, Frida and I met up—as we often did—at the food stalls near our neighbourhood to get some take-out for dinner. Although she'd wanted to eat out, I was in a hurry to get home—I was so excited about something I had to tell her, so it was hard for me to browse through the stalls carefully with Frida.

"Oh, Beib, smell that!" she said, pausing in front of one of the stalls. "Maybe you can make a sauce like that for me sometime!"

I grinned at her and then took a deep whiff of the fragrant air. "Yes, it has chilli and peanuts, I think. I can create something like that for you. Perhaps to go with chicken."

Frida and I liked to taste and smell the different foods sold in the outdoor stalls near our home, as well as in Singapore, where we both still worked. It gave us ideas for meals I could cook for us. I was very practical about my assessments of the foods though, unlike when I'd first started cooking for my wife. Back then, I'd been full of myself, trying to be a chef, trying to make fancy foods and considering myself an artist.

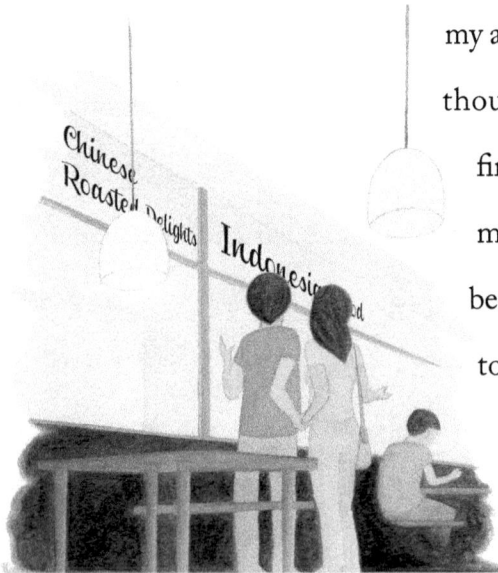

Now I just tried to make the best meals I could for my wife's enjoyment and health. I did not get caught up in labels or in trying to be what I was not, but remained humble in the kitchen, as my father had taught me to be. When we sampled food from the stalls or tasted restaurant food, Frida and I would talk about the ingredients, what worked for us and what didn't, what was good and fresh this time of year, and what things went well together. I did not try to mimic fancier recipes but focused on simple, fresh foods that were locally inspired.

After laughing and chatting, smelling and tasting, we settled on a meal of Padang food with spicy gravy and hot chilli. We carried it home with my feet nearly skipping along with my growing excitement. The next day was Saturday and I could show Frida the special TV I wanted...

I'd been so good about restricting my credit card spending. But the TV we'd brought with us from our old apartment was smallish and seemed grainy compared to the 55" TV I'd discovered while strolling through a local shopping mall. Although money was still tight, I

couldn't resist the allure of that large screen, and I also knew that Frida had never seen how nice the picture was on a big TV. I planned to bring her to the showroom the next day to surprise her and demonstrate the great quality of the showroom TV. I imagined how happy Frida and I would be when we tried the TV out together.

"Beib, you dance along like a child. What is it?" Frida asked as we entered our building and I hurried ahead to press the elevator call button.

Looking up at her with glee in my eyes, I said, "You'll see tomorrow! Let's finish our dinner quickly then go to bed early because I can't wait for tomorrow to come."

Although I noticed Frida's face dropping, I was too excited and full of myself to think about her feelings. I told myself she was just hungry.

Frida was beautiful, with long, dark hair and a shapely figure. As we entered our apartment, I looked into her eyes, hoping to see the bright smile that often lit up her face, the smile I'd fallen in love with, the smile that still flooded my heart with warmth for her. But she was not smiling. Her lips were tightly pressed together and the corners of her mouth turned down in a frown.

A crease had appeared between her eyes, and her forehead was scrunched up with worry. She did not say anything, however.

I'd learned that my wife of few words spoke volumes with her body language. Now I saw that her shoulders were hunched over slightly, her arms pulled in tight, and her hands stuffed into her pockets. She was withdrawing.

In the past, she might have left me there, wondering what was wrong. She would have disappeared into the bedroom, saying nothing. But although we often miscommunicated—usually about money matters—this time Frida found her voice.

"Beib, why don't you tell me what your plan is for tomorrow? You know that I don't really like to wait for such news," she said.

Unable to contain my excitement any longer, I said, "Tomorrow we're going to see how good a 55" TV can be."

"A new TV? Now?"

I had not completely conquered my sudden flashes of anger, although I rarely yelled anymore. But this time, I was taken by surprise. I had expected joy and excitement and

instead got this response. It did not make sense to me, and that made me angry.

"Of course it's time to get a new television!" I said.

"And how will we pay for it? It seems like you're going to start putting too much on your credit cards again."

"Do I not earn more now? Have I not been paying my bills?"

"Beib," Frida said in the gentle tone she used when trying to explain something to me.

I misunderstood her tone to be one of condescension, as if she were treating me like a child, and it made me even angrier.

"My family is doing well! I can spend some money!"

"They are doing well now, but there are still the bills from the hospital and your father's funeral to pay! We still have many debts!"

"Well, you have *seen* me use my credit cards lately. And you have not said anything!"

Though I was still angry, my voice had dropped some in volume because in my heart, I knew that while technically I was right, and Frida hadn't told me not to spend money on my credit cards, she had tried to communicate her worry in her own way. I remembered her reaction was always to say, "okay," when I asked about buying something and I'd taken that "okay" to mean that I should go ahead and make my purchase. Now, it dawned on me that for Frida, "okay" was her way of withdrawing into herself and holding onto her worries. She had not been giving her permission or blessing, she'd been afraid to tell me the truth.

So, now that she was telling me how she really felt, I knew I should listen to her concerns. I should address them calmly. But I was not ready. I'd been too excited to check out the new TV at the showroom the next day. So my anger grew and with it her unwillingness to talk to me about her feelings.

We ate our food in near silence, speaking only of small things, like work, and ignoring the bigger issues looming—like money and our relationship. Quickly finishing our food, we went to the bedroom in silence. I remember lying awake in bed for several hours, steaming mad in the dark.

"That woman is impossible to please!" I told myself.

But as I lay in bed, I thought about how sometimes we are too busy with ourselves, so busy that we ignore little things in our lives. These little things that we ignore can sometimes include little problems—office or work-related problems, for example. And because these are little problems, we ignore them until they compound into something bigger that involves family, relationships, and our overall security in life.

When we ignore our problems, even the little ones, as I had been doing, they all become bigger problems. And then our old ways of dealing with things—avoidance and anger, meanness and dismissal—can come back into play, as they had this time.

This is why we need to look into every problem, every time— to avoid the little things compounding into something bigger. This can only be done by freeing up enough time to deal with life on life's terms, however it may present itself to us.

It may sound easy, but finding valuable minutes to look into the little things can be harder than it sounds. To most people— people like Frida and me who are always on the go—it can really be a challenge. And it is worse for the people who tend to not bother with the little things at all, until of course they become too big to ignore.

I realized I was one of those people who ignored problems until they became big, the way I had ignored the anxious look on my wife's face every time she'd said, "okay," to my spending. And now look what it had gotten me—a big mess.

In the night, my heart shifted. I woke up resolved to work on my issues with Frida rather than ignore them.

Now, I hadn't been making time to cook regularly for my wife. We often ate out or brought food home from the stalls, partly because we liked to try new things, but also because we worked so hard and were tired. I realized that this was part of our problem and that night I had an idea.

The following morning—a Saturday, when we did not have to work—I nudged her and said, "Beib, are you hungry? Can I cook for you?"

She rolled over slowly, looking at me with glistening eyes as if she'd already been crying. My heart nearly broke.

"I don't feel hungry," she said. "Perhaps there was too much spice and heat in that food we ate last night."

Although it was true that my body felt heavy from overeating spicy food, I also knew there was more to my wife's discomfort than the grumbling in her belly. I didn't know what to say, not yet. But my wife's pale face and the way she lay still on her pillow, her hands resting on her stomach, made me think, "Let me see what I can make for her anyway."

I checked the boxes from our take-out and they were empty. So I looked in the fridge. Also disappointing. However, I really wanted to cook a nice breakfast for my wife. I remembered my father's simple omelette and how often that had healed me of both physical and emotional unease in the past. He had never tried to fix problems either by ignoring them, or by taking on airs and cooking something fancy. It was his love for me that mattered most.

So I returned to the fridge, and this time I saw the contents from a different perspective. This time I found that it had a lot of things in it that I could use to cook a dish for my wife. It seemed that when I changed my perspective and my inspiration—no longer to cook a magnificent breakfast but rather to cook something that would please my wife—my brain worked differently. Now I saw not an empty fridge, but rather, some things that I could use to cook, such as eggs, butter, and milk. I'd seen scrambled eggs cooked by some people in TV shows and decided in that moment to cook scrambled eggs. I would use two chicken eggs to create the perfect serving size for Frida.

I heard my wife come up behind me, her stomach grumbling loudly. Looking up, I was struck by how sickly she looked. "My stomach is feeling really weird," she said. "I'm hungry but I don't feel like I can eat anything."

"Relax," I said, looking at her with concern etched in my face but also with gentle comfort and confidence in my voice. "I'll cook the best food for you. Just wait for me in the bedroom."

As Frida shuffled back to the bedroom, my cooking journey continued.

Now I needed to find tools. I've heard great men say, humans need tools to elevate the best that they can achieve. So I turned this way and that, seeking out the best tools that I could find in my kitchen.

First I located the ceramic frying pan that we'd bought when we first moved into our new apartment. I remembered when we bought the ceramic frying pan, we'd seen a cooking demo showing how it used less oil than other pans and learned how the food wouldn't stick to its surface. I had had a bad experience when I'd previously used a coated pan and got black coating surface mixed with my food.

I had felt uneasy about trace metals leaching into my food during the heating process, so I believed ceramic would be the best choice for me. While quite a few metallic types of pots will give off measurable amounts of zinc, cadmium, and bits of other potentially unhealthy chemicals, ceramic pots are normally considered the least reactive of cooking surfaces.

Ceramic pan in one hand, next I rummaged in the drawers until I found a thing that looks like a big wooden spoon with a long handle, a spatula.

"Ahhh," I thought, handling the spatula.

The handle was gently rounded and felt good to hold—sturdy and comfortable in my hand. This is especially important when you have to stir a dish a lot, like with scrambled eggs.

I started cooking my scrambled eggs by putting one

SCRAMBLED EGGS

1 tbsp butter

2 eggs

2 tbsp milk

1 spatula!

Salt & pepper to taste

Keep stirring until the eggs are solid, light yellow and FLUFFY

tablespoon of butter into the frying pan, melting it, and then adding the eggs. I stirred it on medium high heat until the eggs became slightly solid. Then I added two tablespoons of milk and kept stirring until the eggs were solid, light yellow, and fluffy. I scooped them into a simple serving bowl.

I called my wife and she came out from the bedroom, sitting in our dining area and smiling. Her open expression of anticipation and joy reminded me of a child waiting to open a Christmas present. At that moment, that very brief moment, I saw Frida's warmest smile and my own pleasure at seeing this far surpassed any lingering thoughts of the large-screen TV waiting in the mall.

As I served the scrambled eggs, I felt pride at seeing how tasty the golden eggs looked on the plate. I hoped my wife would enjoy the meal because in my heart I knew that I had poured all my love for Frida into the eggs while I cooked them.

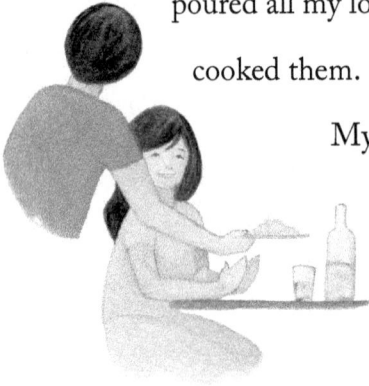

My heart swelled when Frida looked down at her plate and said, "This is so pretty. I can't wait to eat it."

However, although she continued to smile some when she tasted the eggs, the space between her eyes crinkled as though she were puzzled. For the first time, I understood that Frida's facial expressions showed more than she was comfortable saying out loud.

So I asked her, "How does it taste?"

"It's good..." she said, her voice trailing off.

Her face told me there was more that she wanted to say, so I asked again, prompting her—"Oh ya?"

Finally, she blurted, "I think a little bit of salt and pepper would make it better."

I realized then that I had not put any seasoning into my eggs! Shoving back my chair, I ran to the kitchen to grab the salt and pepper shakers and passed those to her. She added some seasoning and tasted it again, tilting her head, thinking and savouring the flavour. I saw in her face that the flavour still wasn't right, and she added some more salt and pepper then tasted the eggs again.

Aha! Now her face brightened like a sunflower in the middle of a garden. In that moment, Frida showed me what she looks like when she's really happy, and, for the first time, I understood, without her saying anything.

"Try some, I can't finish it," she said after a while.

I did, and it tasted really good, and I loved it. After finishing breakfast, Frida's stomach felt better, and with it her mood had improved as well. She helped me to wash the dishes and we enjoyed the rest of the weekend, seeing the TV in the mall but not buying it, and going to the cinema to see a new movie, *Step Up Revolution*, which we chose in the same way we'd chosen to see *My Sister's Keeper* years earlier—it was the show soonest to start that had tickets available. We still loved to choose movies this way, not only because it reminded us of our first real date, but also because it opened us up to seeing all types of movies, movies which generated conversation and thought afterward. After the cinema, we had a wonderful time strolling through the mall arm-in-arm, talking about the movie, about our friends, and about other things that brought us joy.

The scrambled eggs experience taught me many things, perhaps the most important being that I could create an open conversation and slowly build my wife's courage to start speaking her thoughts with more words. I had scolded her quite frequently in the early days of our relationship and more so since our wedding day. I had expected her to speak her mind from the start and never bothered to try and interpret her facial expressions.

But scolding your loved one is never the best way. In our case, my angry admonishments—and I admit, I could be quite unkind in both tone and choice of words—had inflicted psychological wounds on Frida that had made her grow even more afraid to say things to me.

But after I cooked with my entire mind and heart directed at making her the best, healthiest breakfast, I was again influenced by the spirit of cooking. This improved my emotional state so that I was ready to listen carefully. And with my gentle prodding with easy questions, I let my wife know that it was all right to speak more to me now.

⚮

A few weeks passed after I first created and cooked scrambled eggs for my wife. Our communication had improved so much that one fine Sunday morning she said, "I really miss your special scrambled eggs."

That brief sentence lit up my morning and I cooked it for her again. But this time I made sure that I seasoned the eggs with salt and pepper to her taste.

This short sentence from Frida, telling me what she wanted, also became one of my best memories and kept me wanting to cook for her. Not only did that make it clear to me how much our communication had improved, but I now also knew that my cooking skill had improved... whereas before she used to complain that all my food tasted the same, now she craved my food! This was the highest honour and the greatest achievement that anyone who cooks could ever have.

Furthermore, since that morning, I have now scheduled to cook Frida whatever food she craves at least once a week. I know that I still need to do a lot more to improve my relationship with my wife by understanding more about her expressions and her thoughts, and cooking for her helps me to do this without feeling threatened or confused.

Some people say that to really see someone's true form and feeling, we need to make them drunk. But after my scrambled eggs journey, I'd rather say that we only need to cook for someone to understand their true feelings. I have learned so much more about my wife's little expressions. Now I understand when she's being honest with her feelings, when she's being modest, and what the perfect taste for her tongue is.

I can apply that knowledge when I talk or argue with her and become more caring toward her feelings. So now, when I ask about using my credit cards and she says, "okay," but with the same expression on her face as when she'd said "It's good..."

about my unseasoned scrambled eggs, I do not proceed because now I know that it really isn't "okay."

I do not need to yell to understand what Frida wants. I can be quiet and watch for the subtler clues to her feelings. And by using this approach, I have prevented much unnecessary fighting. I had slowly begun to give up my ego to become a better husband, just by scrambling some eggs.

Chapter 5

The Luscious Maple Chicken

Sometimes success brings its own problems. True to the promise I'd made to myself, I'd been cooking for my wife at least once a week for some time. And she'd become more open in her communication with me. She'd even grown comfortable asking me to cook new things for her. Many times, these requests presented a challenge to me and I began to feel as though I were somewhat a victim of my own success. However, mostly I considered these new challenges to be inspiring, and I was grateful for the ways in which they helped me to grow as a cook and as a person.

As I said in the previous chapter, Frida and I often met after work to browse the food stalls either in the market in Singapore, or the one close to home. We'd eat and often pick up fresh ingredients for home. One Tuesday night, after returning from dinner out and shopping, Frida set about cleaning out the refrigerator to make room for some fresh fruit we'd just bought.

She came across a bottle of maple syrup we'd received from my sister-in-law, who lived in Canada. "I want to eat something new, using this syrup," she said. "But not pancakes."

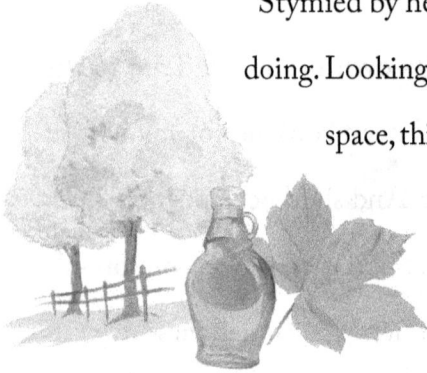

Stymied by her request, I stopped what I was doing. Looking up from my laptop, I stared into space, thinking. I couldn't come up with a single recipe, besides pancakes, that used maple syrup. But as I've said, I'd come to appreciate these challenges.

"Okay," I said after a short while, "let me think about that some more, and I will make something for you this Sunday."

Inside I was both nervous and excited. *What to cook, what to cook...?*

Because maple syrup is not a part of traditional Indonesian cooking, I was unfamiliar with the nuances of its flavour, and so, that night, I slipped into the kitchen to taste it. Tilting the bottle slightly, I dipped my finger into the thick liquid. The first thing that struck me was the aroma, sweet as candy and yet more vibrant, as if the tree from which the syrup came had infused the confection with earth and sunlight.

When I tasted the syrup, I found it to be rich with complex flavours. Because I'd never used it before, I was surprised both by its aroma and by its taste. In my mind, I'd imagined that because maple syrup was sweet, it would be similar to the sweet, Indonesian soy sauce I was used to.

Remembering how my father used sweet soy sauce in the omelette and rice meal he cooked for me when I was a child, I mixed some maple syrup into some leftover rice to see what that would be like.

"Come to bed," called my wife.

"In just a minute," I said, stirring my rice concoction on the stovetop.

I ate a spoonful. Ugh!

It was awful. I went to bed that night still confused about what to cook with the syrup.

The next morning, while I rode the subway to the office, I browsed the Internet on my phone, searching for recipes. I continued my search during lunch that day. It seemed that most of the recipes used maple syrup for roasting meat. Again, I was surprised. It occurred to me that I did not know enough about how flavours combined and that it would help me to do some more research instead of simply copying one of the online recipes I found.

As I chewed my sandwich, I continued browsing the Internet until I came across an article about the "five pillars of taste"— sweetness, saltiness, bitterness, sourness, and umami. This was fascinating, new information to me. I read on.

I learned that sweetness, such as what we find in maple syrup, is one of the five basic tastes a human can experience. It is universally regarded as a pleasurable experience, except perhaps in excess. I found it interesting that the colour of food can affect one's perception of sweetness. For example, adding more red colour to a drink increases its perceived sweetness!

Sweet foods generally give comfort to the ones who eat it. This is, in fact, a basic human instinct, coming from a time when our ancestors had to determine whether berries, roots, and other such foraged food items were safe to eat. Finally, after trying many things, our ancestors decided that if something was sweet, it was all right to eat, and sweet foods became a staple of their diet. To me, sweetness is exemplified by Indonesian sweet soy sauce.

But in the modern world, we have more sophisticated tastes, and not all of us love sweet foods. My wife is one such person. Frida always said that super sweet food hurt her teeth and made them harder to clean. So in order to prepare her the best meal with sweet maple syrup, I knew I would have to moderate the sugary aspect of its taste.

Another of the five pillars of taste contained in maple syrup is called "umami." Umami is an appetitive taste and describes foods with a savoury or meaty flavour. So in addition to adding sweetness to a food, maple syrup will add a savoury hint, which is why it is often used in roasting—it brings out the natural, savoury flavours of the meat. Umami makes me think of a traditional Indonesian meal, Chicken Opor, which is chicken cooked in coconut milk.

This was good to know but umami would not moderate the sweetness of the heavy maple syrup. So I looked to the next pillar of taste, which was sourness. Sourness is the taste that detects acidity in a food. I learned in my reading that sourness also brings out one's appetite. Reading about sourness reminded me of the dried preservative plum my family always eats on Chinese New Year.

Many people—my wife included—cannot eat very much sweet-flavoured food at once. I concluded that adding sourness to sweet food would make the sweet more tolerable for a full meal. Think sweet and sour chicken, for example.

Thus, I decided to use some sourness to make my meal enjoyable from start to finish. I went back to work that afternoon feeling less anxious and more excited about what I might cook that weekend.

When I got home, I went straight to the kitchen and perused the contents of the refrigerator again. I found some spicy, Korean chilli paste, often used to make a traditional Korean cabbage dish called kimchi. This chilli paste is both spicy and sour in taste and even has some saltiness and bitterness from its fermented shrimp content. I also found a bottle of apple juice, which would provide sourness and a tart flavour.

The combination of finding these ingredients and my earlier research on maple syrup and the pillars of taste gave me a surge of confidence. I now had an idea of how I might roast some meat using the chilli sauce and apple juice. I remembered one of my favourite childhood dishes was grilled chicken in sweet soy sauce. I felt inspired and called my wife into the kitchen.

"How about I grill some chicken for Sunday night's meal?" I said.

"Using the maple syrup?" she wanted to know, hesitant at first.

I nodded. "Yes, I have researched how to cook meat with syrup, and I have some great ideas of what to create."

"Could you make it with chicken thighs? I don't like chicken breasts."

"I remember," I said. "Of course."

She hugged me tightly, her hair falling over my shoulder and smelling sweetly of lavender shampoo. I held her tightly, a smile all over my face at how I'd pleased her already without even beginning to cook, just by my intention!

"Thank you for remembering about the maple syrup," she said.

I nodded into her soft hair, joy in my heart.

On Sunday morning, I bought the chicken thighs with some potatoes and thyme. I knew from many of the recipes I'd found that most roast meats and poultry go well with potatoes and herbs. Furthermore, I'd come to use herbs like dill, coriander, basil, and thyme often in my cooking. I will never forget using thyme in my tomato soup, and the welcoming and warming aroma that had wafted through the apartment.

Once we got back home after shopping for ingredients, I created a sauce from ½ cup of maple syrup, ¼ cup of light soy sauce, ¼ cup of sweet soy sauce, one cup of apple juice, one tablespoon of Korean chilli paste, and two sprigs of thyme. After slicing the potatoes thinly, I marinated them in the sauce with the chicken for 15 minutes. Then I roasted it all, with its marinade, at 180°C in the oven for 25 minutes. After that, I served the chicken and potatoes in the marinade, which had been reduced to a thick, delicious sauce. Having learned from my past mistakes when I'd served without tasting my creation first, I sampled my dish. Perfection!

After I served the dish to my wife, she sniffed the aroma of the piping hot food and smiled warmly at me. "Wow!" she said. "You really made something new for me. You know at first I was worried you'd just say 'No,' to my request. Like whenever I ask you if I can buy something new."

Remembering the couple's cup my wife had wanted to buy early in our marriage and several purchases I'd denied since, I bowed my head. Not because I'd declined to buy these things so much as the manner in which I'd refused—by scolding and recrimination.

"I'm sorry," I said. "But you must never be afraid to ask for what you want. Perhaps I won't always be able to provide it. But we should never stop communicating, as we have been doing so well lately."

MAPLE CHICKEN

Make a sauce with

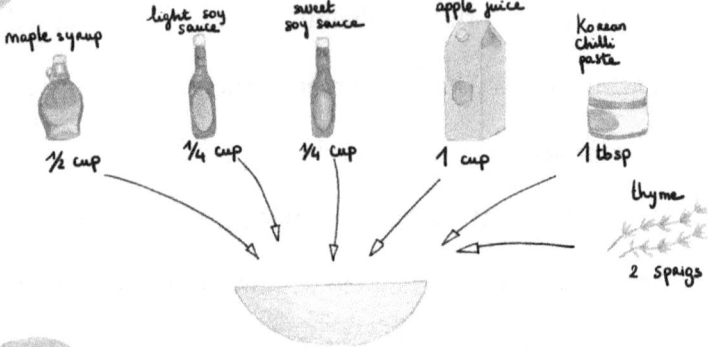

maple syrup — ½ cup

light soy sauce — ¼ cup

sweet soy sauce — ¼ cup

apple juice — 1 cup

Korean chilli paste — 1 tbsp

thyme — 2 sprigs

Marinate

thinly sliced potatoes

Chicken thighs

in the sauce for 15 minutes

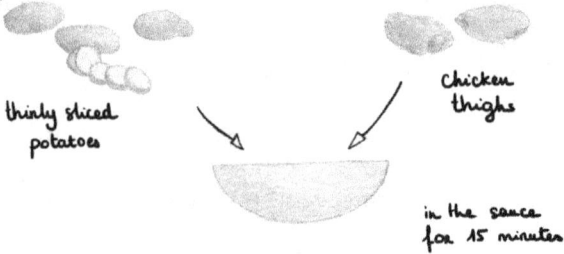

Roast it all with the marinade in an oven for 25 min.

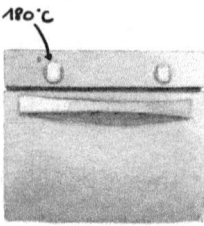

180°C

"Yes, we've come a long way. And thank you for this meal," she said, nodding.

"Thank *you* for the challenge," I said. "It inspired me to create a dish that is truly mine for you."

Placing a forkful of food into her mouth, Frida smiled her biggest, most generous and warm smile. When she'd finished chewing, she said, "Beib, this is wonderful. It is the most tender roast chicken I have ever had. And it has the perfect balance of sweet and spicy that I love."

Watching her face as she ate that night was the greatest thanks I could get. What a gift Frida gave me by enjoying my food so thoroughly! Better than anything we could buy. And after that night, the maple chicken became a regular request from my wife, a request I've been happy to honour.

I had, in creating this meal, considered all of the five pillars of taste—sweetness, saltiness, bitterness, sourness, and umami. Some of these I've discussed already. Saltiness

came into play as well, through the fermented shrimp in the Korean chilli paste and the light soy sauce.

Bitterness, the only one of the five tastes I have not yet addressed much, was something that, in fact, I thought a great deal about in building my recipe. I remembered the taste well from the bitter gourd my mother used to cook when I was little. In my recipe, there was some bitterness in the fermented shrimp found in the sauce but I felt that it was more addressed by the addition of thyme to my recipe. The unique bitterness of the thyme I used, with slightly lemony and minty notes, worked well in counterpoint to the sweetness of the maple syrup.

Some additional notes about bitterness in recipes:

1. **Bitter food helps to absorb nutrients.**

   While bitterness is often perceived as unpleasant, the interaction between bitter constituents in foods and our bitter taste receptors stimulates the production of gastric acid in the stomach. This helps prime the stomach for the food it is about to encounter. "Bitter foods and herbs help to stimulate digestive juices and support food digestion," says professional dietician Nicole Dube of Halifax, Nova Scotia. "Bitter foods help stimulate our taste receptors on the tongue, which subsequently stimulates enzyme production and bile flow. The better your food is digested, the more nutrients you will absorb from your food. It doesn't matter what you eat, if you can't absorb it, it won't be of much benefit to you."

2. **Bitterness balances taste buds and controls that sweet tooth.**

   Bitter foods are thought to reduce food cravings and aid in weight loss because bitterness controls our appetite in eating sweet food.

3. **Bitter food cleanses the body.**

   Bitter foods contain sulphur-based compounds, which support the natural detoxification pathways in the liver, helping it to do what it is meant to do—keep your body clean and clear. Bitter food also stimulates better metabolism.

Learning so much about bitterness in food and about all five of the pillars of taste would not have happened if it were not for my wife's challenge: to create for her a meal using maple syrup, an unfamiliar ingredient to me. And when I met this challenge,

I learned that it taught me lessons not only about cooking this one meal. The experience turned out to be representative of life to me, as cooking foods has often been. Creating the maple syrup chicken dish taught me much about challenges in general and how to handle them.

First, I found that by accepting the challenge, I became more open to both my wife and to learning new things, such as the five pillars of taste and the various flavour combinations. It brought what I already knew into my present situation when I recalled the pillars in terms of foods I'd tasted before, while at the same time opening me up to new flavour experiences.

But I believe the openness with which I faced this culinary challenge was most important in how it affected me overall, as a person. Only an open-minded and open-hearted person can accept others' challenges. And overcoming challenges can only happen by embracing them. By embracing them, I don't mean to take in what is already the status quo, but rather, to face them with courage, strength, and resolve. Accepting challenges—even ones that may seem trivial, such as what to cook with maple syrup—has its own rewards:

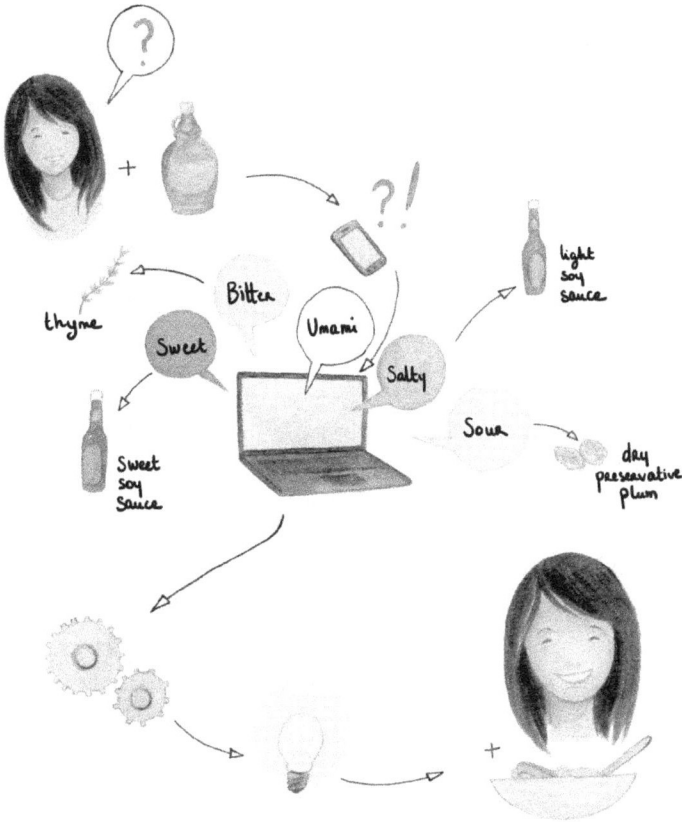

1. Challenges present us opportunities for growth. No one ever learned their deepest lessons in easy circumstances. Ask around. Our deepest growth happens when we are stretched.

2. Challenges reveal our limitations and offer us a platform to rise above them. The solution often lies in what we consider the "problem." Look again!

3. Challenges teach us the necessity of learning more, as I found in my research for the best recipe based on my wife's request.

4. Challenges humble us. This kind of humbling becomes a blessing when we respond with the desire to learn. The humble are teachable.

5. Challenges remind us that life is not all about ourselves. It becomes so easy to lose sight of the big picture when life happens on our self-centred terms.

6. Challenges are the stepping stones we need in order to become successful. Every human being will be tested by life's challenges. Often we think that in order to cope, we must avoid life's tests. But challenges do not go away. We cannot ignore them and think they will pass. Rather, as I've said, we must embrace them. "Lean into them," as a friend of mine says.

Life's challenges help us develop into mature, stable, and purposeful human beings. When we meet challenges, we stimulate the mind to believe that nothing is impossible. The challenges we face are meant to sharpen your faith, focus your mind, and re-align your integrity and character. Deep within, I

believe we all have what it takes to embrace any and all of life's

challenges. And when we learn to confront and successfully

overcome these, we will become more confident in the face of

future challenges.

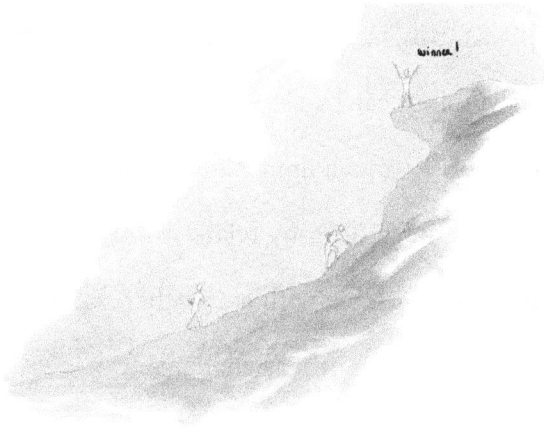

I learned all of this through facing challenges in cooking,

and I have adapted it to all areas of my life. I have also found

that the world of challenges deals with two types of people.

One type of person is the "victor" and the other type is the

"victim."

Let's take a look at the positive type of person—the victor. The

victor realizes that when a challenge presents itself, that this is a

winner's challenge. The feeling is not one of being overwhelmed,

but rather one is inspired and excited, similar to what I felt after my wife's request for a meal made with maple syrup.

And I did "win," in many ways, from meeting Frida's challenge. For one thing, at that time, I did not yet have a recipe that was truly mine. After creating my own chicken recipe—that is to say, accepting my wife's challenge—I ended up with the first recipe that was truly mine… the first of many more to come.

And my winnings can be counted in so many more ways than my culinary skills. So much more happened for me. I gained new openness inside me and in my relationship with my wife. We became more comfortable with each other, vocalizing requests and trying to meet each other's challenges.

I also became a victor and a winner in other areas of my life. Being a victor has helped me in my job. For example, previously I had never been brave enough to do a presentation at work. It

was a challenge that often presented itself that I was too afraid to meet. But after successfully cooking challenging foods for my wife and explaining my creations when I served them, I gained the confidence to present my ideas to my bosses in my office. I now receive more opportunities and take greater satisfaction in my work.

The victors—those who overcome challenges and win— are people who excel and continue on their journey of success. They prepare their minds, they use self-help tools to boost their confidence levels, and they do not give in to fear. They constantly find solutions and this grows their faith in themselves. Negative thoughts are not part of their pattern of thinking.

Consider, instead, the "victim." The victim type broods over adversity and becomes awash in negative thoughts. Victims pile up reasons and excuses why life is so bad to them. They become overwhelmed easily, and thus they cannot muster up the courage to meet the simplest of life's challenges. The victim continues to spiral downward, as challenges—which might also be seen as opportunities—come and go, leaving the victim behind but carrying the victor forward to success.

Thus, for me, cooking is a way of life. And cooking the luscious maple chicken I made for my wife has changed my life positively in ways I've only just begun to experience.

CHAPTER 6

The Heritage French Toast

SINCE creating the maple chicken recipe for my wife, I continued to take on more cooking challenges. Sometimes I would even ask Frida for a challenge.

"What would you like to eat this weekend? I'll cook it for you," I said as we rode the subway home from work one Friday night.

Tired from a long week of work, Frida untied her hair, letting it hang free. The sweet scent of lavender from her shampoo floated through the air, enveloping me and making me smile, warmth and love for my wife filling my heart.

"What are you smiling at?" she said with a grin.

Pecking her on the cheek, I said, "You. I will always smile for you. Now, tell me, what meal should I cook this weekend?"

"How about some of that chicken like you made last week?"

I shook my head, took her hand and kissed her fingertips. "No, something new. Challenge me."

"Oh Beib, I'm too tired to think. Maybe you'll get inspired at the market."

I shrugged—maybe I would. If not, perhaps something on a cooking show would give me an idea, or I'd remember a meal from my childhood that I could now make my own... the possibilities were limitless at that time in my life, limitless in what I might cook and equally rich in what Frida and I might make of our lives.

This is not to say that after making the maple chicken, my cooking life became easy. In fact, I learned that taking on challenges was much easier said than done! Not all my cooking adventures ended in success. Far from it... I'd say that only about one in ten meals came out well. Some of my attempts were failures of such magnitude, I remember them to this day—

Burnt Paella with rice so hard it still tasted like grain.

A Padang stew I burnt so badly that the bottom of my pot cracked.

A pineapple upside-down cake, also burnt, and too bitter to eat.

Whenever a meal would turn out badly, whenever I felt like a failure as a cook, I would recall what cooking show host Guy Fieri said about cooking:

"Cooking is like snow skiing: If you don't fall at least ten times, then you're not skiing hard enough."

It helped me to remember that only by overcoming one's failures does one achieve success. Cooking is a lifelong process and effort. It should be a journey, like love, like life itself.

I know from experience that this can be hard to keep in mind. It has certainly been something with which I have struggled. Oftentimes, especially after a great cooking failure,

I wanted to give up and only buy food from the stalls near my apartment. I would take long breaks from cooking, licking wounds that festered with self-pity and criticism.

But I came out of those times stronger and more determined to succeed than before. Sometimes I brought myself out of my fear of failure because I didn't feel right when I wasn't cooking regularly. Other times, I resumed cooking because of other people, nudging me back to my rightful place in the kitchen, cooking for my loved ones.

I remember one time when I hadn't cooked for about a month following a failed dish. I was sulking around the apartment, snapping at Frida, and feeling down. The phone rang.

It was my mother, calling to tell me that it had been exactly one year since my father had passed away.

"I have been thinking about him all day," she said. "Remember the omelette he used to make you? Remember the pork he used to cook for you and your sister? He loved to cook for his family."

I felt a pang, like a small knife piercing my heart as images flashed through my mind of my father chopping vegetables; of my father in his tee shirt and shorts, standing over the hot stove; of my father with his eyes at half-mast, so tired from working in his shop all day, and yet rising whenever he saw that I was hungry, rising and smiling, and going to the kitchen to cook for me… Sure, he had his failures in the kitchen just as I had mine, but it never stopped him from continuing to cook his best for his family.

As my mother went on, reminiscing about my father, I remembered one thing in particular that my father cooked, a very special treat—a dessert. For some, dessert is a regular part of mealtimes. For us it was a privilege we didn't always enjoy.

We were poor. My parents struggled to provide even the most basic necessities. After school and supplies were paid for, there was little remaining for extras, like toys, or even clothes. My sister and I typically wore hand-me-downs from other relatives, clothing that was sometimes faded or ill-fitting, but was the best we had. As for toys, I remember I had a Teenage Mutant Ninja Turtle action figure that I played with for many years, even after one arm had fallen off.

So while we did not go hungry, dessert after meals was a luxury my parents could not really afford. Still, I remembered how my father almost always found a way to transform some cheap and simple ingredients into something special for us. One such ingredient was a loaf of bread.

At nine PM, just before closing up his own shop, my father would go to the convenience store next door and wait in line to buy a loaf of day-old bread at a discounted price. Listening at the door between our home and the shop, I would hear him chatting with some of our neighbours, having a good time while he waited. He was charming and gregarious and loved to talk and laugh with the other shopkeepers.

When he returned, he ruffled my hair and said, "I managed to get some cheap and delicious bread. Now we can have our dessert. Come, Gus."

Although it was quite late by then, my sweet tooth kept me awake, and I followed my father to the kitchen. He checked the refrigerator to see what other ingredients we had. As usual, there were only some chicken eggs. But my father did not see that as

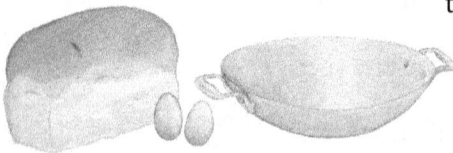

a drawback, only as a challenge, which he was happy to meet.

Beating the eggs, he added sugar and then dipped slices of the white bread into the mixture. Using only an aluminium wok with which he always cooked, he fried the bread. The warmth in the kitchen was nothing compared to the warmth in our hearts whenever my father made us his fried bread. We all knew the loving spirit he put into everything he made.

So, although we were poor, my father protected my sister and me from feeling our poverty. He sugar-coated our reality just as he sugar-coated the day-old bread and turned the mundane— and our lack of money with which to buy fancy things—into sweetness that filled our bellies and our lives. My father always made sure that we had good food to fill our childhoods with happy memories. We could not feel poor in his presence, only rich with his love.

～⌀

One Sunday, a fall morning in the middle of our rainy season, I woke to find the wind blowing hot and humid through the bedroom window, rattling the windowpane and whipping the curtain up so that it billowed out like a dancing ghost. Glancing next to me, I saw that my wife was still sleeping. I felt my heart grow warm and soft, watching her sleep. I loved her so much!

As I got up to close the window before the rain came in, I thought about my recent cooking failures, and how I'd been avoiding the kitchen lately. In so doing, I'd been holding back my love for my wife as well. I decided in that moment to forego any new recipes for a time and instead to focus on cooking foods I knew well, such as recipes from my childhood—foods which I remembered my father using to express his love for his family.

My wife had bought some bread the day before, and it was out on the table, three slices remaining. Remembering my father's fried bread and what comfort and joy it had brought to my sister and me, I knew I had to make that for Frida. So I got an egg and some margarine out of the refrigerator. I also had butter, but my father had always used margarine.

As usual, I used the frying pan that my wife and I had bought when we moved into our first apartment together. I felt a surge of confidence, standing taller and yet more relaxed whenever I used this pan. I broke the egg into a bowl and added half a teaspoon of salt and white pepper and one teaspoon of sugar.

FRENCH BREAD

Break one egg and add

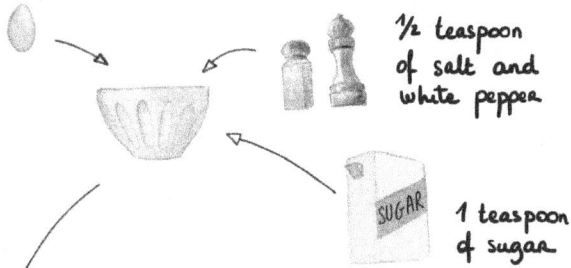

½ teaspoon of salt and white pepper

SUGAR

1 teaspoon of sugar

Stir until it becomes runny and spread onto slices of bread

Fry with margarine

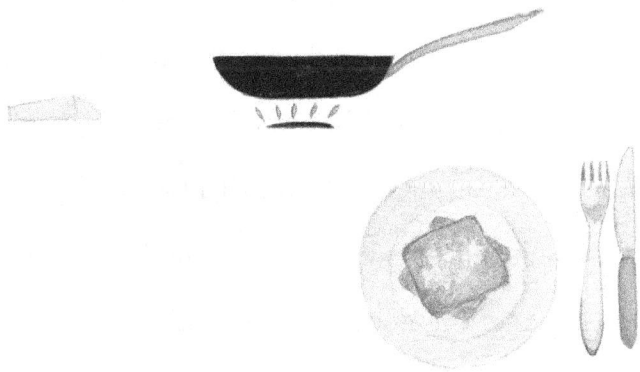

I stirred the mixture until it became runny, then spread it onto my three slices of bread. When I'd finished frying the coated bread with margarine, I stacked the slices on a serving plate and cleaned up all the tools that I'd used.

"Wow, I smell something delicious, and I'm starving," my wife said as she approached the dining room table, still wearing her pyjamas.

I'd just finished washing the dishes and now joined my wife at the table. We ate the fried bread together, hardly talking, just savouring the food I'd cooked for us.

"The weather is so nasty out, I didn't want to get out of bed," Frida said. "Now I'm so glad I did! This bread is so warm and sweet. I can also taste the savoury flavour of margarine. When did you learn to cook this?"

Realizing I'd never told her the whole story of my father cooking for me as a child, I enjoyed sharing the story, recalling the warmth of my father's food. The rest of the morning, with the scent of my fried bread lingering in the air, I took Frida with me on a journey from my childhood to the present through tales of my father's cooking. The stories were powerful and moved her almost to tears several times.

This sharing of food and my history added a new depth to our relationship. By understanding my family culture and heritage, my wife could now appreciate the values of my family even more, values that always included the procurement and enjoyment of good food, no matter how difficult our situation was. In retelling the stories of my childhood, I learned that love is timeless. And one of the best ways to share timeless love is through cooking family recipes, so that the love from the previous generation is felt by the next generation.

After finishing our breakfast, Frida told me, "I really love this French toast you made for me."

This was the first time that I'd heard the fancy name of my father's recipe. I'd only ever known it as "fried bread."

Continuing my story, I told my wife how my father would

cook it for me whenever I craved it. As it was whenever he cooked for me, it didn't matter whether he was tired or had problems on his mind. It did not matter whether we had money. Only his constant, unwavering love for me mattered.

Because it was so representative of my childhood, I said, "We will call it Heritage French Toast."

As I cleared the dishes from our breakfast and as the wind howled outside and rain pelted the windows, I continued to tell my wife stories and truths from my youth. I explained how poor my family had been... How my father had kept his shop open until nine or ten at night, in the hopes of attracting a few more customers. How my sister and I had worn hand-me-downs from my aunt's family, and how we were often teased at school for our obvious poverty. I told Frida about the scarcity of toys and the one-armed Ninja Turtle I'd played with for ten years... and explained, with tears in my eyes, about the significance of the empty, money boxes my mother had found after my father's death.

The more I talked, the easier and less shameful it became. I told Frida how whenever my father had saved enough profit from his shop, my mother would go to the market to buy one pack of Padang rice with curry gravy and one piece of meat to be shared between me and my sister. And in the end, how all this scarcity in my childhood had led me to overusing credit cards as an adult… because those pieces of plastic money were like magic to me.

I remembered and told Frida how a salesperson had once said to me, "Just use your credit card now, and pay the minimum payment later. That way you can enjoy all the pleasures of owning what you want right away."

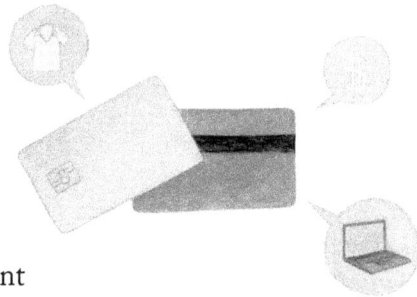

In that statement I heard, "One swipe and you can have all the fancy stuff that you've ever dreamt of without worrying about money anymore."

Nodding and taking my hand, Frida kissed my fingertips. Her lips were warm and soft and filled me with a rush of love that felt like a flower blooming in my heart.

"Thank you for sharing this with me," she said. "Now I understand why you overspent with your cards. And I'm more grateful than ever that you don't do that anymore. It must have been very hard for you to stop on your own. I only wish you'd told me this sooner so that I could have helped you."

Smiling, I held back tears of joy. "Thank you for being so patient with me."

And so, the Heritage French Toast did more than warm our bellies. It allowed me to walk through the pain still lingering from growing up in poverty. By sharing this pain with my wife, I released its hold on me. At the same time, I opened the lines of communication between Frida and me even more, allowing us to grow in our love and trust of each other.

A little while later, while my wife was straightening up the apartment and I was on my laptop catching up on some emails, Frida said, "The bread was cooked so nicely. I can still feel the wonderful crunch of the edges in my mouth!"

Smiling, I said, "You liked that? That was my own addition to the recipe. My father couldn't make it crunchy because he only had an old aluminium wok to cook in."

"What did you change to make it so crunchy?"

Smiling proudly, I said, "I'll show you."

I went into the kitchen with Frida right behind me. I pointed to the ceramic frying pan. "This pan that I bought when we first moved in is what did it!"

In that moment, the notion that superior cooking tools improves one's cooking was reinforced in me. In this case, because the ceramic coating of the frying pan distributes heat more effectively than aluminium, for example, it causes some protein-rich foods, such as eggs, to cook more quickly. The ceramic also retains heat and distributes it evenly. So ceramic pans won't burn food with high sugar content, such as bread. Instead the ceramic quickly makes the egg-coated bread crunchy when it is used with margarine and medium high heat.

As I've said, this experience with what Frida and I renamed the Heritage French Toast brought me many gifts. It improved our relationship, and it helped to release me from the pain and shame of childhood poverty. Most importantly, it taught me a great deal about timeless love.

The way I see it now, the tradition of enjoying great food from one generation to another is one form of timeless love, that is to say, love that continues on through time—as my father's love for his family was passed down and then regenerated in my love for my own family. The food that has been brought down from one generation to another gifts us with an emotional experience of food.

In her seventh book, *The Way to Cook*, Julia Child writes, "Dining with one's friends and beloved family is certainly one of life's primal and most innocent delights, one that is both soul-satisfying and eternal."

Thus, family recipes are a way of keeping our ancestry alive. Food appeals to all five of our senses and because of this, it can evoke vivid memories of our childhood, of our relationships with family members who have passed away, and of who we ourselves were, during any given time in our lives. Food reminds us of experiences long forgotten and allows us to relive feelings of comfort, satisfaction, or excitement. Preserving family recipes allows us to access these emotions anytime we choose, whether it's during a holiday or on a simple occasion we want to make special.

By cooking family recipes and passing them down to the next generation, we create a legacy of food dedicated to those who came before us. Documenting and improving family recipes keeps our relatives and loved ones alive in our hearts. Then, if each successive cook in a family contributes his own flavour and style, we merge the past with the present in a very special way.

Laurie Colwin writes, "No one who cooks, cooks alone. Even at her most solitary, a cook in the kitchen is surrounded by generations of cooks past, the advice and menus of cooks present, the wisdom of cookbook writers."

As we record the thoughts, ideas, and processes of our traditional family meals, we create an heirloom that will be handed down to our children, grandchildren, and great-grandchildren. We build a bridge by which our loved ones can learn about who we are, even after we are gone from this world.

This is important because part of knowing the path ahead is to understand where you've come from. The legacy of recipes passed down from one generation to another is a tool, a family tree of foods, a line that can be traced for decades into the past and the future.

In the end, the heritage of food also makes a new family closer... Food is a universal need, eating is something all human beings do. Because of this, throughout the ages, meals have been a symbol of sharing, nurturing, and loving one another.

Remembering, collecting, recording, and passing down the recipes your loved ones have left to you is a wonderful way to honour and immortalize your family. Not only will these recipes allow you to create meals that are a meaningful experience to your loved ones today, they will also inspire you to create your own versions of dishes, to add your own flavour and style. Something you will, in turn, pass on to the next generation of your family.

Take what your heritage has given to you and infuse it with your own meaning and power. Use your past to enrich your future. In my experience, family ties are bonds that stand the test of time, which is why I say that foods passed down to us are representative of timeless love. Preserving family recipes is a way of saving and honouring our heritage so that future generations can continue to feel that love and strengthen those ties.

CHAPTER 7

The Golden Aloo Gobi

In all traditions, food has been celebrated in one way or another.

As chef Samia Ahad has said, "Food is at the centre of some of the most important moments of our lives. It is over the dinner table that memories are made, deals are conducted, and pain is shared. Over food we bond, we fight, we mourn, we romance, and we celebrate."

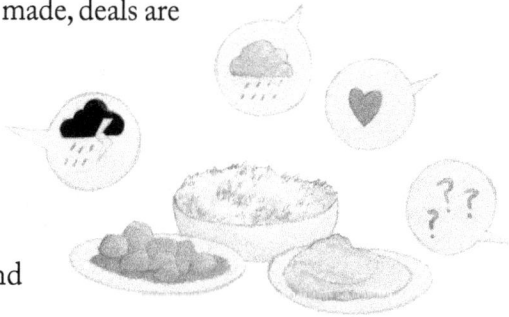

I've written about the importance of food memories and passing down recipes in former chapters. Our pleasant memories of meals past, combined with revisiting those meals and adding our own perspectives and inspiration to the recipes make up what I call, "food tradition." It has been food tradition that has motivated me to keep cooking for my loved ones.

Tradition doesn't always have to represent the old ways or old things from our lives, things we've learned from the lives of those who have gone before us, though it can mean those things. But we can also create new traditions, which we then pass on to our families and friends…

"I'm ready to go out for dinner if we have to," I remember my mother saying during a visit to Singapore.

Emerging from the guest room of our apartment in tee shirt and slacks, she ran a brush through her short, black hair. "But I am tired of eating at the food stalls. What if you cooked for us, Gus?"

My family visited my wife and me in Singapore for a week out of every year, and we always ate out at restaurants or at the food court near my apartment. Formerly, I'd only shared recipes with my sister when she visited me because she was interested in cooking, as I was. But at my mother's request that day, I was, as always, up to the challenge—and the joy—of cooking for my family. Getting out my trusty ceramic frying pan, I prepared the marinade while Frida and my mother went to the market for chicken and some vegetables to put on the side. We enjoyed the maple chicken I'd created for Frida some months earlier for dinner that night, and thus, a new tradition was born!

Since then, I have cooked other foods for my mother, my sister and her husband, and my mother-in-law. I have also shared many recipes with my sister so that she could adapt them to her family's taste buds, thereby creating her own traditions.

But as I've said, food tradition does not necessarily always come from our own experiences. Often, we may absorb the traditions of another into our own. This is similar to a marriage where two people from different backgrounds—each with their own traditions and culture—come together and form a union that later on produces their own traditions and passes these traditions on to their children.

This happens even when the couple comes from very similar backgrounds. We cannot assume that just because our partner went to the same high school, was raised in the same town, or possessed the same culture and worldview, that he or she will naturally do things the same way we do—for each individual has experienced these things in his or her own way. Therefore, we each come to a relationship with different ways of doing things.

No two families bring up their children exactly the same way; therefore, couples will have to articulate what they expect, what they are used to, and what they would like to see happen in their own marriage in order to have unity. On the points where my culture clashed with Frida's, we've been afforded the opportunity to search within ourselves to find common ground. We've had to learn how to critique each other's cultural presuppositions without being judgmental or offensive.

By honouring and respecting the traditions each of us bring to the table, we can help each other to grow. We point out

blind spots, drawing out the best of each of our cultures to form a new version. We can then celebrate a richness of diversity in our new family.

As with all traditions, food traditions come from many sources, and we will do best if we accept and adapt to the new foods that our friends or our spouses introduce to us. By choosing not to be afraid or repelled by traditions that are different from our own past experience—by choosing instead to absorb the cultural experiences and input of others—we learn to live in harmony with our loved ones and our fellow person. And, eventually, we get to transform these food traditions passed on to us by others into our own cooking. This happened to me with an Indian dish I created for my wife…

It was several months after I'd recreated my father's fried bread into what Frida and I now called Heritage French Toast. We were walking through the outdoor market, savouring the aromas of different food when the smell of curry wafted through the air.

"I remember you told me about how your father bought one pack of Padang food with rice and curry gravy for you and your sister," Frida said. "And you told me that you loved it. Correct?"

"Yes. Why?"

"The smell of that curry got me thinking… You love to eat curry too? Because I was the only one who ate all the curry gravy whenever my parents bought it and they would scold me for it. 'It isn't healthy,' they always said. But I ate it anyway and now I'm craving it."

"We can buy some and take it home," I said, reaching for my wallet.

"I have a better idea," said Frida. "How about you cook that Padang food curry for me?"

Immediately, I balked. "But I have never cooked it before," I said. Although I was learning to accept challenges, my confidence was low at the time, due to some recent failures in the kitchen. "And even if I had, I wouldn't remember how to cook it again."

Frida smiled and squeezed my hand to show her faith in me. "Any curry will do," she said.

I nodded, trying to remain motivated and get inspired. Once again, I felt frustrated and stymied. But as we walked home, I suddenly recalled a food memory from a happy time, a time several years earlier when my colleagues and I had taken an Indian friend out to lunch.

I remembered the table, covered in a bright cloth, filled with bowls and dishes of more curried food than I'd ever seen before—red curry, yellow curry, and brown curry. I said to my friend, Kunwar, "I've never eaten Indian food before. It's a little intimidating. Does it all taste good?"

Clapping me on the back, Kunwar said, "Every bit of it! It reminds me of home. Try it. You'll love it!"

And so I filled my plate. Again and again! Kunwar was right, the food was delicious, and the flavours stayed in my deepest memory, connected not only with the good taste on my tongue but also with the wonderful time my friends and I all had at that luncheon.

My favourite dish was a cauliflower curry. It was spicy and unusual, but I adapted to the strange taste quickly, and by the end of the meal, I loved that

particular dish so much, I would search for it every time I ate
at an Indian restaurant after that. However, I'd never asked about
it and didn't even know what it was called, much less how to
cook it myself.

Remembering that delicious Indian meal, I now said to Frida,
"How about an Indian dish? I believe you'll love it. But let me
find the recipe first."

With a shrug and her trademark, warm smile, she said, "Sure,
I would love to try that."

This truly was a challenge. The next day, I browsed the
Internet but had no luck finding that delicious cauliflower curry
dish that I remembered so well. I really had no idea how to find
any of the kinds of dishes I'd tasted and loved at that luncheon
long past with Kunwar. I tried to find the cauliflower dish in
some Indian stalls and restaurants near my apartment, but it
seemed that none of them cooked it anymore. Or perhaps I
didn't describe it well. In any case, they were unable to help me
when I stopped to ask about the dish.

I was frustrated and worried, unwilling to disappoint my
Frida—or myself—and yet unsure what to do next. Then,
one night, I watched a cooking channel and there was Chef

Michael Smith, cooking the very dish that I'd been searching for! I learned that the dish's name is Aloo Gobi. It is a dry Pakistani, Indian, and Nepali cuisine dish made with potatoes (aloo), cauliflower (gobi), and Indian curry spices. Turmeric gives the dish its yellowish colour.

Watching and learning that night, I felt that I had found true gold in others' tradition that I wanted to transform into my own recipe to make it a tradition in my family.

The following weekend, I got my supplies at the supermarket— onions, cauliflower, potato, minced chicken, curry powder, cumin seeds, chilli flakes, turmeric powder, and butter. I had decided to add minced chicken to make the dish more appealing and filling. Once I got the ingredients, I followed what Chef Michael Smith had shown in his cooking video, changing some ingredients as I went to make it simpler for me to create.

First I cooked about ¼ cup of the butter for about 5 minutes, until it was nicely browned and fragrant. I added two minced onions, one tablespoon of curry powder, one tablespoon of cumin seeds, one tablespoon of turmeric powder to enhance the yellow colour, and one teaspoon of chilli flakes. Then I cooked this all for only about 2 to 3 minutes more, just enough to heat the onion and release the seasoning flavours. I then added the

minced chicken breast together with the three diced potatoes

and one cauliflower and tossed it all to coat it thoroughly with

the pan mixture. Finally, I seasoned the dish with salt and some

more curry powder to satisfy my wife's taste buds based on my

experience back when I'd made her scrambled eggs and she'd

added her own salt. Adding water and covering the pot, I lowered

the heat and simmered until everything was tender, about 12

to 15 minutes. I served my Aloo Gobi variation with the pot's

lid still closed.

Frida sat at our modest table with fork in hand, waiting to

eat. Her face was open and smiling, but her anxiety was clear

in her furrowed brow. She wanted so much for this dish to turn

out well for me, and even before serving her, I felt myself glow

under the light of her love for me.

"Voila!" I said, removing the pot's lid, "the golden Aloo Gobi!"

My heart raced as she tasted my food. Although I felt proud

of my accomplishment and fairly certain I'd succeeded with this

dish, the tasting was the true test.

I needn't have worried.

"The curry taste is incredible," she said. "The spiciness is perfect!"

ALOO GOBI

1/4 cup of butter

Cook for about 5 min until it is nicely browned and fragrant.

Add

2 minced onions

1 tbsp of curry powder

1 tbsp of turmeric powder

1 tbsp of cumin seeds

1 teaspoon of chilli flakes

Cook for about 2-3 min

then, **add**

3 diced potatoes

1 cauliflower

minced chicken breast

Toss it all to coat it with the pan mixture

salt to taste

water

Add water and cover the pot. Simmer until everything is tender (about 12-15 min)

And then, more important than her words, she continued to eat. She took some steamed rice leftover from lunchtime and spooned the Aloo Gobi on top of it. With the heat of the curry making us sweat, we still finished every bit of my Aloo Gobi down to the last drop of curry gravy. Afterward, we were so full, we stayed at the table, rubbing our warm bellies and savouring the after effects of a delicious meal that would remain in our memories and become a new food tradition for us.

We not only felt the warming power of the herbs from the curry powder, but we also enjoyed the benefits of curry powder flowing through our bodies. Traditional curry powder is filled with spices that help the digestive system. Black pepper, a common ingredient in most curry powder blends, promotes stomach acid secretion and reduces intestinal gas. Bay leaves promote proper digestion. Cinnamon is an antidote for an upset stomach. Cloves treat indigestion. Coriander helps relieve stomach-aches and treats digestive upsets, and cumin helps with digestive issues.

All of this warmth, great flavour, and the flow of good health within us made us blush with happiness. I remember being somewhat in awe that something as simple and necessary as food could make my wife and I feel so alike, so connected. I flushed not only from the heat of the meal, but also from joy, and I could see that she was fulfilled and joyous as well.

At this point, I realized that while enjoying good food, we didn't have to pretend to be someone else in front of each other. And this is what friendship in marriage is. Think about it—the word "friendship" conjures up thoughts of honesty, vulnerability, companionship, and mutual respect. It also implies a certain outlaying of time and energy. All of this was present in our Aloo Gobi experience, from Frida trusting me to fill her desire for a spicy curry, to my patience in finding the right recipe, to eating and enjoying the same food together.

There's a saying, "Love is patient; love is kind. It always protects, always trusts, always hopes, and always perseveres."

I remembered when I was young and liked a girl, my parents advised me, "Be a friend to each other first."

It took me quite a while to understand both of these quotations—and how well they went together—but, finally, I realized the truths in the saying and in my parents' words...

Most of the time, we can stand to be more patient toward our friends. And one of the best parts of friendship is that we don't have to be pretentious.

This is not always true when we treat our spouses differently than how they truly should be treated—as our best friends. But if we accept our partners as our friends, in their true forms, we can easily respect each other, trust each other, and persevere for the sake of each other's happiness.

The kind of love that has grown from friendship can be revealed through cooking for our spouses. In cooking the best food for our loved ones, we have to be patient. We have to be kind to understand their needs. We have to be trustworthy so that they will enjoy the food that we cook. We have to always be hopeful that our food turns out nicely. And we have to persevere in our research, trying many recipes to get the best results to suit their taste buds.

Understanding friendship has gone a long way in helping me understand how to better love and be with my spouse. Once Frida and I became true friends, we accepted each other's flaws and foibles—as well as strengths and accomplishments—which has been a natural path in elevating the relationship in our marriage and in making our marriage last.

Commitment and chemistry are ingredients you don't want to leave out of the recipe but without friendship you can't bake the cake!

To be friends with your mate means:

- You respect him or her.
- You treat him or her like your equal, even when your upbringing and your own selfish ways try to convince you otherwise.
- You talk about how you feel and think about both the good and bad in your life together.
- You even risk conflict by being more honest than you are comfortable with because it builds intimacy in your marriage.
- You plan and dream together because life is too complicated to just wing it.

In other words, you treat your partner like your best friend.

Marriage is a challenging and rewarding relationship, and so often we forget that "I do" is only the beginning. In real life, sometimes your Disney fairy tale ends up feeling more like a Wes Craven horror flick. It seems today that the institution of marriage is becoming more and more a matter of convenience rather than a strong binding commitment between two people who are dedicated to each other.

Our society, and even the world, has become desensitized to divorce, when just 50 years ago getting a divorce was a scandal. Today it's widely accepted and not looked down upon with the same level of scorn and shame that was once so typical.

Today, marriages need more than just the right set of

circumstances and financial solvency; great marriages require that both spouses put in realistic effort. And it is wiser for each one of us to produce his or her own best effort first, not waiting for our spouses to make the relationship work. When we pour our energy into someone, the other person will return that effort with even more commitment, love, and energy of their own.

When you love someone—*really* love them—they know it! Make sure that your love is always on display, and cooking can be one of the best ways to show love to your spouse...

Because when we serve the food that we cook, it will show how humbly we serve our spouse and how much effort we put forth in preparing the food. In the end, the food that touches your spouse's tongue will touch his or her heart as well.

Furthermore, in cooking, we can learn how to forgive each other. The most important part of any good relationship is forgiveness. Whenever I failed to cook good food for my wife, she learned to forgive me and I also learned to forgive myself. This forgiving process has been, for Frida and me, the route to self-healing that in time has led to us accepting each other's defects and loving each other as we are, allowing each of us to relax into our true selves.

Do not despair if none of this comes easy in your own marriage. Remember, it has not in mine either. Any relationship is difficult. You are two different people with different backgrounds and different points of view. This has the potential to cause difficulties; however—and more importantly—these differences also have the potential to bring you closer. The way is simple—*never give up on your spouse*, and make the best of the tough times because those times create the best chances for a sturdier foundation.

Never, ever give up!

Making your marriage more rewarding is an investment in your future happiness. The more effort you put into your marriage, the more benefits you will reap. I find that in tough times it helps to remember the things that attracted me to my spouse in the beginning, opening my heart to the passion that my wife and I once had. I remember that kindness evokes kindness and love attracts love. I always work on my relationship as though it's the most important thing in my life, because, in the end, it's the only thing that really matters.

Through my parents' example and based on my experiences with my Frida, I've come to believe that if you try to do as I do, loving your spouse and committing to bettering your relationship in any way you can, your family will be happier, your children will feel more secure and have a better foundation for their future, and you will have a newfound respect for yourself. Focus on building a better relationship and you will thank yourself in the end.

CHAPTER 8

The Friendship Steak

A great marriage begins with great friendship. After the first blush of new love has passed, if we are friends with our spouses, the relationship will continue to flourish. Since we are naturally our own best friends, we should also treat our loved ones, from family to friends to spouses, as well as we would ourselves. It's just as the old saying goes, "Treat others as you would treat yourself."

Feeding ourselves healthy foods is great self-care. And giving our spouses—and friends—pure, nutritious, and tasty whole foods manifests how much we care for them. As will.i.am said about cooking for someone else:

"It's not good cooking for yourself; the joy is in cooking for others—it's the same with music."

I live by that quote, and cooking food is the music that I make for others, especially my wife. It is not only because she is my spouse. It is also because of my sincere belief that food will nourish and build greater friendships, and Frida is my best friend.

That said, it isn't always easy to know what food will best nourish and satisfy our friends, even our spouses. Each of us has our own favourite food. And we also have our own staple foods. A staple food, sometimes simply referred to as a staple, is a food that is eaten routinely, and in such quantities that it constitutes a dominant portion of a standard diet in a given population. Staple foods vary from place to place, but typically they are inexpensive or readily available foods that supply one or more of the three organic macronutrients (more about these later) needed for survival and health.

Frida and I grew up in different families, in different cities, each with different staple foods. For example, she grew up in

Jakarta, in a family with a strong Sumatran background passed on from her father, so Frida prefers sour and strong tasting foods. I, on the other hand, grew up in Central Java and I prefer something sweet rather than sour foods. So we often differ on the flavours we love. However, Frida and I also grew up with some of the same staple foods, such as rice.

Remember, Frida and I love to eat. We share an adventurous nature with regards to food. So, after we got married, we did not confine ourselves to traditional foods that reminded us of home, but rather, explored many other foods, foods that are easily accessible in Singapore. Foods that come from many different cultures—Japanese, Korean, Western, and more.

However, we still each enjoyed different flavours, flavours reminiscent of our childhoods. Frida, as I've said, likes sour foods. I prefer sweet. Nevertheless, neither of us feels full unless we include rice—our shared staple food—in our meal. Rice makes both of us feel satisfied no matter what else we eat with it.

However, after moving to Singapore, I worked on losing weight by eating less food during lunch and dinner, and

eating healthier, more nutritious foods, such as fruits and cereals. And, knowing that many people trying to lose weight avoid carbohydrates, I cut rice out of my diet as much as possible. I also changed my lifestyle, going to bed earlier and then rising earlier in the mornings and generally keeping busier.

During my early days in Singapore, these lifestyle changes were difficult. I felt a void in my life; I did not have a sense of purpose, nor anyone with whom I could share my joys and sorrows. These voids in my life translated into an emptiness inside that I longed to fill with food. But when I started to embrace opportunities to socialize more, and to open up to others, I no longer felt so empty, which translated into a smaller appetite and thus a smaller waistline. When I finally became good friends with Frida, weight loss became almost easy because being with Frida filled me in a way that I had never felt before. It was, essentially, friendship that made me feel complete and full without needing to gorge myself on food.

Although I never forgot my craving for rice, the staple food from my childhood, once I'd established a beautiful life surrounded by my friends, I learned to enjoy other foods without any rice. My fulfilment came not from food, but from eating

together with the people that I cared about.

I did not—and still do not—feel the need to eat rice with every meal. Not so with Frida. Though she will sometimes suppress her desire for steamed rice so that we can enjoy the same meal together, most of the time, she asks for rice to come along with her dishes. But more about rice later... first, I'd like to further address friendship in food.

I believe there is already friendship in every food, and the best cooks or chefs are the ones able to enhance that inherent friendship. They do this not only by creating pleasing flavour combinations, but also by the skilled use of "macronutrients."

Nutrients are needed for growth, metabolism, and other body functions. Macronutrients are nutrients that provide nutritive calories, or energy. And, since "macro" means large, macronutrients must be eaten in large amounts.

There are three macronutrients: carbohydrate, protein, and fat. The best recipes will often use a combination of these three nutrients on one plate. For example, to accompany roasted chicken recipes, we include a potato salad with some gravy, thereby providing carbohydrate, protein, and fat from the chicken, potato, and gravy. We use all three macronutrients because each serves a different purpose:

Carbohydrates are broken down into simple sugars, which stimulate the body to produce insulin. Insulin is necessary to move sugar from the blood into the cells, where it is needed for energy.

Protein is a building block for the body. It is used to make and repair many different tissues, as well as to make many hormones, enzymes, and chemicals the body needs to function.

Fat provides long-term energy. When the body is short on carbohydrates, the body breaks down fat for fuel. Fat also helps the body to moderate its energy usage, creating lasting, consistent energy, rather than short bursts followed by exhaustion or the immediate need for more food.

Carbohydrates   Protein

Macronutrients work together to provide energy, cell growth and healing, and warmth to our bodies—all of which make up what we call good health. Nevertheless, we also need to be careful in combining foods with these nutrients in order to prevent digestion problems. Furthermore, as I learned in my early days in Singapore, it is not only the nutrients in our food that sustain us—but it is also the company we keep.

And so... we return to friendship in food. As I said, when I first moved to Singapore, I felt empty inside. Later, I began hanging around with colleagues from work and other friends who I met through them. Four or five of us would get together on the weekends, going to dinner and the cinema, or out to a coffee shop or club. Just as macronutrients work together to provide what the body needs, my friends and I brought different personalities and strengths to the table, each of these necessary to our good time and overall fulfilment:

Rizal (a.k.a. Akie) knew us all and was the icebreaker between us. Without him, we would have felt strange being together, but he made us all comfortable.

Haryati (a.k.a. Ameh) was the one with whom you could stay up with until four AM, just talking.

Marselina (a.k.a. Acim) was the organizer. She guided us toward what to do when we got together.

Frida was great fun to be around, quick with a laugh, and easy to smile with. She encouraged us to have a great time and to be ourselves with each other.

I gave the best suggestions on relationship issues and I tried my best to make each of us feel special, heard, and understood.

Each of us had something important to offer the group. Still, as with macronutrients in food, our strengths could be bad for our overall enjoyment if our personalities weren't moderated. Too much of a good thing can ruin a situation. For example, I remember that sometimes a few of us would be more talkative than the others, and that made the rest uncomfortable. The whole atmosphere turned awkward when there was too much of any one of us.

It is the same with food combinations—if we put too much fat or oil in our food, it will taste bad; if we put too much carbohydrates (rice, potatoes, or bread) and proteins (meat, poultry, etc.) in our food, it will disturb our digestive systems. We want our loved ones to enjoy our food and to feel good and healthy after eating, so we must strive for the best combinations for taste and well-being when cooking for them.

But as I've learned from experience, understanding and the ability to create great food—to cultivate friendship in food properly—can't be achieved by a one-time cooking occurrence. One should research recipes that others have used, as well as study flavour and nutrient combinations. And then… well, I believe that practice makes perfect. The beauty of practicing cooking as much as possible is that we learn by doing, and through doing we come to understand different food ingredients on many levels, from first taste to lasting impression.

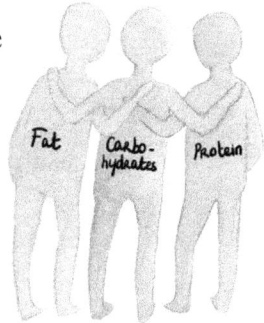

My father taught me this when I was a child, first by eating his food and later through cooking for him. And I practiced these principles when learning to cook for my wife.

After successfully cooking some great dishes for my wife based on food traditions passed down from my family or friends, I began to grow in confidence. I began to understand how food ingredients could be good friends with each other or could instead be hateful enemies, creating a disastrous taste. But I wanted to learn more.

I started to look at Frida's and my staple food. Even though we share a staple food—rice—I realized that I had never cooked any rice dish for my wife. Because I wanted to cultivate our friendship through food, I decided that I should serve a meal that was really satisfying to my wife. And what she craved with her meals was always steamed rice.

So I was already thinking of including rice in my next meal when I asked my wife, "What food are you craving today?"

Frida looked up from her magazine. "Oh, I'm glad you asked because I'm starving! A steak would be really good right now but maybe make me two—I'm really hungry. Or even something that would be nice to eat with steamed rice."

I was taken aback by her answer, as I'd expected she'd want rice, but considering her first response was steak, I was puzzled because I'd never cooked steak with steamed rice before.

"Steak" in Singapore refers to the cut rather than the type of meat. So as I walked to the kitchen to see what we had in the refrigerator, I asked, "What type of meat do you want?"

"Anything will do as long as it's good and makes me full."

Well, that was no help, I thought, still stymied by the idea of cooking steak with rice. Leaving the kitchen to get my shoes, I decided to go to the nearest supermarket and see what meats looked good and to find something that inspired me.

Because I was still determined to cook a rice dish for Frida, I said on my way to the door, "Why don't you cook some steamed rice and I'll get the meat for the steak."

My wife was quite surprised. She knew I could be resistant and lacked confidence when I'd not cooked something before. "Steak with steamed rice? Really?"

Shrugging as if this were nothing new to me, I said, "Sure, why not."

Frida gave me an encouraging smile and headed for the kitchen to make the rice. I watched her for a moment, feeling glad that at least that part of the meal would be good because I knew that she was really good at preparing steamed rice.

Through the archway to the kitchen, I saw her take one small cup of rice and pour it into the rice cooker with two cups of water. She used the same cup for measuring the rice and the water. She then turned on the rice cooker and I knew that the rice would be ready in 50 minutes. I'd better hurry!

It took me half an hour to return with my steak ingredients. I planned to cook something fast because once the rice was done I had to be ready to serve my steak too. So I chose pan-fried salmon steak.

To cook the salmon, I simply put some butter in my favourite ceramic frying pan together with one smashed garlic clove and one spring of rosemary. I spread some olive oil onto one of the salmon steaks and seasoned it with salt and pepper. Once the butter melted, I laid the salmon in the frying pan with the skin on the bottom to crunch it up. While one side of the meat cooked, I used the dining spoon to slowly scoop up the hot butter in the frying pan and pour it on top of the salmon over and over again until the first steak turned cloudy pink.

SALMON STEAK

Season the steak with

olive oil, salt & pepper

Melt some butter with 1 sprig of rosemary

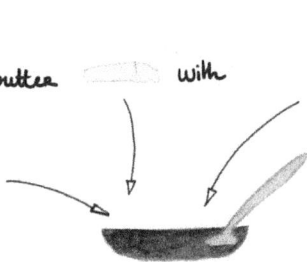

1 smashed garlic clove

and lay the salmon in the frying pan with the skin on the bottom.

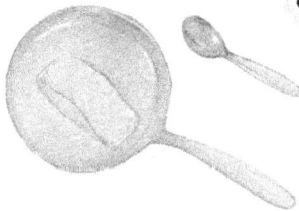

Scoop up the hot butter with a dining spoon and pour it on top of the salmon over and over again until it turns pink.

Serve with plated steamed rice.

Just as I finished frying the second salmon fillet, I heard the rice cooker signal that the steamed rice was ready. Perfect timing! I smiled with pride at my accomplishment.

While the steaks rested a short while, I decided to enhance the steamed rice by adding a bit of a twist. I remembered that a few nights before, my wife had seemed so happy while eating some sushi rice. So I decided to try recreating the same taste for her.

Opening the rice cooker lid, I poured Mirin onto the rice, stirring it thoroughly. Once it was mixed, I closed the rice cooker lid and left it for one minute. While waiting for the rice to absorb the Mirin, I prepared dining plates. While doing so, I glanced up at my wife, who waited—impatient already—at our small, dining room table. Nodding at her, I smiled to let her know that the food would be ready soon. I could tell she was feeling anxious by the way she nervously tidied up the table while she waited, straightening the papers and other things that always accumulated there in the centre of our apartment.

Mirin is an essential condiment used in Japanese cuisine. It is a type of rice wine similar to sake, but with a lower alcohol content and higher sugar content. It has a slight sweetness and sourness in it.

This is the perfect condiment for Frida and me, because even though most of the time we disagree on those two taste pillars, a great friendship between sourness and sweetness already exists in the Mirin. Furthermore, traditionally in Japan, Mirin has been used to add a bright touch to grilled (broiled) fish or to erase the fishy smell. So I was certain that adding Mirin to the rice would create the best friendship between my salmon steak and Frida's rice.

After the rice absorbed the Mirin completely, I plated the rice so that it became the base to hold the salmon steak. Once the rice was arranged properly, I laid the salmon steak with the skin side up, on top of the rice.

As I served it to my wife, I whispered, "Hope you like it."

My wife's eyes glittered with expectation and her face lit

up with a big smile. I knew at that moment that she was really looking forward to tasting what I'd made for her. She even took out her phone and began to take a picture of the salmon steak.

Laughing, I nudged the phone out of the way. "Come on… Come on… Let's eat."

She picked up her fork. "I really didn't expect a rice dish when I said that I craved a steak," she said. "But you pulled it off! I'm so happy you delivered both the steak that I asked for and the steamed rice that I always love to eat."

As I sat next to Frida at the table and ate my own steak, I glowed with pride. There's nothing better than enjoying the staple food that has been our tongue's best friend since we were just babies. And the food is even more meaningful when we put more effort into making it, as I did by adding the Mirin. With this experience, I also understood that to honour our staple foods, we should also honour the culture of the people who enjoy it.

Watching Frida out of the corner of my eye, I saw how much my wife was truly satisfied by this simple dish. I could almost feel her taste buds sing and her stomach fill with joy. I now understood why, previously, she'd always asked whether my dishes were good to eat with rice.

My friendship steak and rice was a great success on many levels. I'd pleased my loved one, and, ultimately, I'd managed to build an intercultural friendship with my food.

CHAPTER 9

The Organic Unity of Guacamole

THERE are many ways to go about learning to cook good food for your loved ones. As you've read here already, I've tried many of these approaches with varying results. For example, I have studied the elements of good meals, examining and dissecting others' recipes and researching what more experienced chefs have said about cooking. I have learned by searching my past for useful food memories. I have tried new foods, exposing myself directly to the traditions of other cultures.

I have worked long and hard at creating friendships in food and in life. I have worked at my communication skills and on my relationship with my wife through words and honesty.

These are all useful skills; however, my purpose in writing this book is not to tell you to work harder at creating friendship and a good relationship with your spouse. It is to reveal what my experience has shown me to be a better way. That is, instead of working on fixing a problem directly, it can be just as helpful—or, in my case, more so—to work hard at cooking better food. The rest will follow. I sincerely believe that if we concentrate our effort on improving our cooking, our food will naturally create what we call an "organic unity" in our relationship with our spouses. Of course, many activities that we do for and with our spouses develop organic unity, but I am a cook, so let's talk about cooking…

I rode the subway to work every day with my wife. It was a long ride—more than an hour—and while we often talked during the ride, sometimes we just sat together, listening to music on one of our phones, each of us with one earbud. One day, as I enjoyed the organic unity of sharing music with Frida, my mind wandered to considering

organic unity in food and guacamole came to mind.

Guacamole is an avocado-based dip, or salad, first created by the Aztecs in what is now Mexico. There are hundreds of ways to make guacamole to suit different taste buds. Different ingredients result in vastly different tastes and textures in guacamole. However, as I realized that morning, if there's no organic unity in your dip, this simple and versatile dish will fail.

Basically, "organic unity" means that a thing is made up of interdependent parts. Aristotle describes organic unity in creative writing by explaining how it relies internally on narration and drama to be cohesive, but without balance between the two sides, the work suffers. I love this description and believe that this kind of unity should also happen in food, especially in food with a lot of ingredients to combine, such as guacamole.

Since we have already talked about the five pillars of taste and friendship between the three macronutrients, let's now take our understanding of ingredient combinations further, using guacamole as our example. Other than making an organic unity with taste and nutrients, good guacamole should also consider the three pillars of food texture: soft or hard, mushy or crunchy, and smooth or lumpy. Texture is crucial to the enjoyment and acceptability of foods. Would you enjoy a mushy apple or soggy toast?

Chef Mario Batali says that the single word "crispy" will sell a restaurant dish quicker than any number of clever adjectives. Picture "aubergines" on a menu. You might hesitate to order them, fearing they would be flaccid or oily, as they so often are. Now think how much more appealing "crispy aubergines" sound. "Crispy" makes everything appear as safe and crunchy as chips. So the texture of the food that we cook really affects our willingness to eat it.

Professor Peter Barham, from Bristol University's School of Physics, has studied the many factors affecting perception of flavour and texture. He has worked with chefs such as Heston

Blumenthal to develop recipes rooted in the scientific, molecular properties of food. Barham says there are surprising factors that can affect the texture of food. For example, what people touch affects how they perceive texture.

Andy Taylor, formerly of the University of Nottingham and who is now working in the food industry, has experimented with changing the texture of a standard meal. He blended and re-formed a meal of fish and chips. The flavour was the same but he removed its visual and textural properties. The meal was (not surprisingly) perceived as inferior by those testing it.

As I came to understand these facts, I realized that texture has a unifying effect on food. Texture merges flavourful taste and macronutrients, creating an organic unity such as that described by Aristotle—that is, power from each ingredient combined with balance between all.

As I've said, Frida and I have come a long way in growing an organic unity in our relationship. We communicate more deeply; we share activities and interests; we spend most of our free time together. We are best friends.

That same Friday after work, as I waited for Frida to join me for the trip home, I found myself thinking more about texture in food—the research I'd done—and also about Frida and me. A smile creased my face as I realized how rich and varied the texture of our life together had become. For the most part, we'd successfully merged the elements of work and play, sustenance and frivolity, communication and reflection. And it was good.

I looked up to see Frida approaching, her heels clicking on the concrete floor of the platform. "What are you smiling about?" she asked.

I shrugged. "You. And me."

Kissing my cheek, she said, "Well, that's good. What would you like to do tonight, Beib?"

The train rumbled into the station. Over the squeal of the brakes I said, "I'm tired and don't really feel like going out like we usually do."

Normally, we'd eat out on a Friday night, but I'd been working at a new job that required me to return to work often in the middle of the night. I was exhausted. When Frida climbed aboard the train without answering right away, I worried that I might have disappointed her by saying that I wanted to stay home. However, organic unity revealed itself in the answer she gave as we sat in our seats—

"I don't want to go out tonight either," she said, squeezing my hand and laying her head on my shoulder. "I've had so many customers' complaints to deal with at work. I'm exhausted. We've both been working so hard. Let's eat at home."

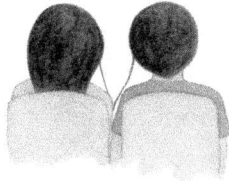

It was settled. Both of us were content to just go home, shower, and cuddle up on the couch to watch TV with some take-out dinner. I was the master of the remote and chose a Mexican cooking channel.

"Are you feeling adventurous?" Frida asked with a grin.

She knew that, as much as I loved to experiment in the kitchen, I could still be intimidated by new ideas and recipes. Smiling back at my wife, I recalled something Chef Michael Symon had said—"People come up to me all the time and say,

'Oh, I love to watch Food Network,' and I ask them what they cook, and they say, 'I don't really cook.' They're afraid, they're intimidated, they know all about food from eating out and watching TV, but they don't know where to start in their own kitchen."

Nevertheless, we should never stop before we start. This is a motto I live by.

After all, every master chef was once a disaster too. It helped to remember that. Furthermore, I reminded myself, if the recipe on a show felt overwhelming, I could do as I'd done—simplify it in my own cooking. I could make it my own.

It is also said that courage is to be afraid and yet to try something anyway, so I told Frida, "Maybe. Or maybe not adventurous. Courageous."

Indicating the chef on TV, she replied, "Good, because that guacamole he's making looks really refreshing. And you've never made guacamole before."

"Would you like to try it?"

She nodded eagerly.

"Then I'll make it for you tomorrow."

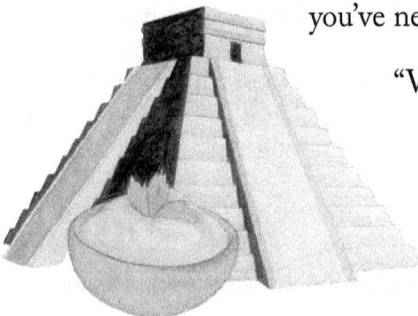

The next morning, we went to the nearest supermarket to gather all the ingredients needed for making guacamole. Walking through the vegetable displays, I saw some ready-made guacamole and chips. But to use prepared food would be neither adventurous nor courageous. Besides, those didn't seem up to my wife's standard. I wanted to fulfil my promise to my wife to make her fresh guacamole, refreshing and satisfying, like what we'd seen on TV.

Continuing to search for ingredients, I found some wonderful, ripe avocados, dark green in colour, the bottoms of them soft to the touch. Avocadoes are the main ingredients of guacamole and actually have a specific importance: in food-science terms, they act as a "covalent bond" with other ingredients. The creaminess of the fruit converts disparate tastes into complementary ones and punches up otherwise drab ingredients. For example, grilled corn kernels, diced red onions, and mango elbow each other for attention until chunks of avocado mediate and mellow the mix into a tasty salsa—thus turning an unstable structure into a stable one. An ordinary salad of greens, tomatoes, and raw vegetables turns almost decadent when slices of avocado are included.

In guacamole, avocado shows its best bonding power by

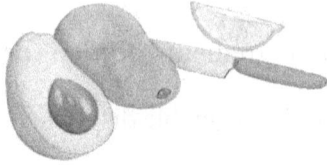

binding together many varied vegetables into one big, flavourful snack. And what could be more fun than having a flavourful but healthy snack? I happily put the best avocadoes I could find into the basket.

While I gathered this primary ingredient, Frida sought out the rest of what I'd need. Appearing in front of me as I laid

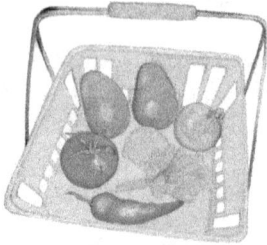

the avocados gently in the bottom of our basket, she showed me what she'd found: an onion, a big red chilli, tomato, lime, and coriander.

It all looked fresh and delicious, still, she looked concerned. "I'm not sure," she said, "But I feel like we should also put something savoury in the guacamole."

So I decided to get some sliced smoked bacon and blue cheese.

On the way to the checkout counter, I remembered one more thing that I'd almost forgotten. Chips, to dip with. I remembered the instant guacamole and bag of chips and how that hadn't seemed right. Right then, I decided it would be better to enjoy the guacamole with my own homemade chips. At the end of the row of packaged chips, I found a pack of flat bread. Inspired, I picked up the bag of pita bread, certain that I could make something out of it to complement the guacamole.

I continued to reflect on my wife and my growing organic unity as we paid for our food. Those few minutes of shopping together made me realize that it wasn't just the food that brought us closer—even shopping for ingredients had become a shared adventure. Unlike earlier in our relationship when I'd overspent with my credit cards trying to prove my worth to Frida, shopping for guacamole ingredients that day we only spent a few dollars, and we really enjoyed the experience in team building.

There are a lot of ways to get to know your spouse. And let's face it: no matter how much you think you know already, there are always more things you can learn about him or her. Human beings are vastly complicated creatures. That morning, my wife and I found out how much fun it was to discuss the food ingredients that we saw, talking about our likes and dislikes. It was a simple, cost-effective, and unique way to get to know each other better.

The most successful marriages are those where a husband and wife learn how to function as a team, lean on one another's strengths, and also support each other in times of weakness or strain. One person may become the captain of the team in a given situation but this captain must act as a wise leader, recognizing his own and the other's strengths and using them for the benefit of the entire family. Then, some decisions may be made jointly, or by each spouse in his or her area of expertise. Either way, your goal as a couple should be to make decisions that strengthen and benefit your relationship.

This is what I experienced when grocery shopping with my wife. I was the one who knew the guacamole recipe that I wanted to make and we agreed on it; then I let her find many of the best ingredients because I knew that my wife was meticulous about picking vegetables.

Heading home, I was lost in thought about how I should prepare the best guacamole for Frida, and I didn't talk much. But since the trip from the supermarket was about 15 minutes by train, I had plenty of time to think of a recipe. When we arrived at home, I went straight to the kitchen. I took out the tools I required and began.

First I cut up the pita bread into triangles. Using my trusty, ceramic frying pan, I fried the chips in oil, and then cooked the bacon to create a crunchy bite inside my guacamole. Then I scooped the avocadoes out from their skins, and mashed them with some lime juice to prevent browning and add some citrus flavour. After that, I diced and mixed all the vegetables, blue cheese, and crispy bacon into the avocado mixture, and served it with my crunchy homemade flat-bread chips.

Although it is always warm in Singapore, it was the most humid season of the year. We kept the windows open instead

GUACAMOLE

Cut the pita in triangles
and fry it in oil

Cook the bacon

Scoop the avocadoes out of their skins
and mash them with some lime juice

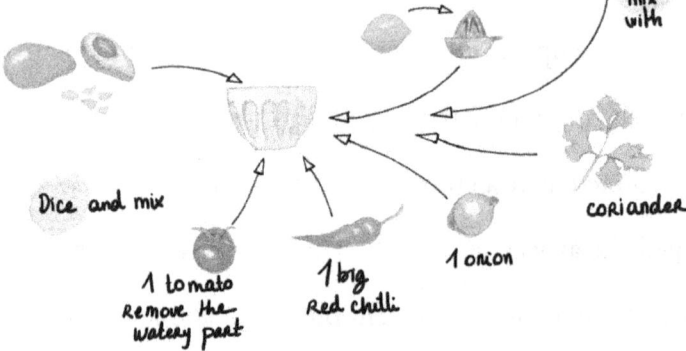

Dice
and
mix
with

Dice and mix

coriander

1 tomato
Remove the
watery part

1 big
Red chilli

1 onion

Serve with
the crunchy homemade
flat bread chips.

of running the air conditioner, and the weather had my wife sweating while she waited for me to finish cooking. Still, she looked eager and excited, which further raised my confidence. I proudly brought my new recipe—my own version of traditional Mexican guacamole—to the table.

Frida looked amazed. "I can't believe you created that recipe just from what we saw on the show last night."

I grinned. "It wouldn't be great if you hadn't picked the best ingredients."

Now she looked proud as she said, "Thanks. I learned from you and from my own research about the benefits of organic produce. So I put it into practice. I chose the freshest and plumpest vegetables I could find for this guacamole."

Sitting next to each other at the small table, we enjoyed the guacamole and crunchy flat-bread chips together that afternoon. We found it to be as refreshing as Frida had hoped for. Even more refreshing to me was the look on my wife's face while she savoured every bite of it.

As Aristotle said, organic unity requires balance overall as well as

strong parts. And with this experience I learned not only how guacamole fulfilled these requirements, but also the importance of organic unity in my entire cooking journey. All parts of creating a meal, from inspiration to execution, must be strong, so that in the end, the best food will result. If my wife hadn't chosen the best vegetables for my guacamole, everything would have tasted bad and it wouldn't have been as refreshing. If I hadn't chosen to add good homemade chips, the guacamole wouldn't have been as pleasing in taste and texture. Adding the additional ingredients, blue cheese and bacon, further elevated the guacamole. And none of this would have been possible if we hadn't shopped together.

Frida and I had finally found an organic unity—in our food and in the texture of our lives.

CHAPTER 10

The Wrap

My cooking practice has led me to many wonderful things and brought about many changes in my relationship with Frida. For example, on my wedding day I'd expected an easy life before me, one filled with laughter and love. I soon learned that love didn't always come with laughter—sometimes it brought tears and frustration.

As I've written here, my early days with my wife were not easy. Frida and I have experienced ups and downs, like any married couple. In the beginning, before I discovered the joys of cooking for my wife, I overspent with my credit cards, trying to please and impress her, as well as to fill the hole that gaped inside me whenever life was not progressing as I'd planned or hoped.

Frida and I fought often in those early days. We experienced the difficulty of living together under one roof, attempting to share a life, while coming from very different upbringings. Our parents had different styles of parenting and this led to Frida and me having different points of view on almost everything. Bringing harmony to our two, often opposed, mindsets was a daily challenge.

And because we hadn't yet learned to communicate, we thought we were fighting about money, and jobs, and other material things. True, those were problems, but the deeper issue truly was rooted in our miscommunications.

It is never an easy task for a married couple to learn to live together and to communicate well. Certainly, we struggled. But as I began to use cooking as a tool, I grew in my ability to listen and to speak my mind calmly and reasonably. My willingness inspired Frida to do the same. We found ways to fill the holes in ourselves and to help each other to grow and change.

I remain motivated in resolving any miscommunications through cooking, and I am now able to move past a disagreement to the next issues that arise, no longer remaining fixated on the same old argument, over and over. This is important because as one of my old friends said, "The sign that your relationship is improving is not when you stop fighting, but when you fight for different reasons because you have moved on and settled the previous issues. When you do this, you begin to realize that the fighting itself doesn't mean your relationship is bad. It is only growing. Your relationship is only going downhill when you fight again and again over the same thing."

After I began cooking for Frida, our communication improved. Sometimes my disagreement wasn't so much with her as with the food itself! Sometimes it was with both at once. For example, one of the problems that I faced as I cooked for my wife more frequently was being unable to find friendship with a food that she loved and vice versa. As I've written, I worked hard to understand flavour, studying taste and texture. But understanding doesn't always lead to friendship right away.

One of the five pillars of taste that gave me the most difficulty was sourness. I grew up in a family who loved food rooted in sweetness and umami (savoury). On the other hand, my wife grew up in a family that most appreciated sourness, especially from vinegar. One vinegar in particular that I never much liked, yet my wife loved, was balsamic vinegar.

Balsamic vinegar has a tricky taste and a wide range of selection. It can be very cheap but also very expensive. In an effort to help me find friendship with balsamic vinegar, Frida and I tried several different types of common balsamic vinegar found in our supermarket. My wife liked them all, usually simply mixing the sour condiment into her salad. But somehow, I couldn't agree with the flavour. And as my father had taught me, as long as I couldn't be friendly with a certain food, it would be difficult to cook the best dish using it. So this balsamic vinegar certainly caused me a great headache.

I knew that communication between flavours was important, just as communication was a cornerstone in my relationship with my wife. Thus, in an effort to cook pleasing food for her while still meeting my own desires, I tried to bring my childhood love of sweetness into harmony with balsamic vinegar... I tried and failed, again and again. It was just like having the same fight over and over, and I knew my cooking was not growing. Whenever I tried to create a dish with balsamic vinegar, my wife would say that it was too sweet and that the balsamic flavour had been lost because of the sweet condiments I'd tried combining with it. But if I didn't do that, *I* didn't like the meal because it was too sour.

I tried to eat balsamic vinegar with bread, but it was too sour. I tried it with vegetables, but it wouldn't stick to the vegetables and was too runny. I tried to make a balsamic-based sauce by mixing it with chicken and pan-frying it, but it only flavoured the outside of the chicken, leaving the meat tasting unseasoned. I grew more and more frustrated with each attempt to find friendship with balsamic vinegar. It hurt my confidence and even made me start feeling a little sad, a little of a hole inside, reminiscent of when my wife and I had miscommunicated in our early relationship with each other.

One fine Saturday afternoon, Frida and I strolled through a shopping mall. She noticed a booth promoting balsamic vinegar.

"That booth is quite interesting," she said. "Perhaps there you can find a balsamic vinegar you will like."

I shrugged, unconvinced but willing to have a closer look.

Frida noted that the promoter was also selling some olive oil with unique flavours, such as pumpkin seed. "I believe they also sell some good balsamic vinegar. Ask the man."

So I did—I was willing to try anything! The promoter smiled encouragement as he offered me samples of his balsamic vinegar. Right away I saw that this vinegar that I tasted was quite sticky, almost like a syrup, very unlike the consistency of the supermarket balsamic I'd had before, which was thin and runny.

I was amazed to find that on just the first trial, I had already—finally—found the taste that I had been seeking for so long. It was rich and complicated. Though it was sour enough, it also tasted sweet. These two pillars of taste popped separately in my mouth yet combined beautifully. The promoter explained that the balsamic vinegar in his stall was, actually, a traditional balsamic vinegar, created using a traditional fermentation process to produce such a complex flavour.

I learned then that traditional balsamic vinegar is different in so many ways from the usual balsamic vinegar found in most grocery stores. For example, the promoter said that the usual balsamic vinegar has a short fermentation period, for example only a few years, or even worse, that some might not use *any* fermentation to create the sourness but might be just a mixture of synthetic ingredients. But the traditional balsamic vinegar that I tasted at the stall was produced from real grapes with a fermentation time of twenty-five years to create a complex taste that I loved.

Traditional balsamic vinegar is the granddaddy of balsamic vinegars. To this day, it is only made in Reggio Emilia and Modena, Italy, using Old World methods, and production is overseen from beginning to end by a special certification agency.

It begins with grape must—whole pressed grapes complete with juice, skin, seeds, and stems. The must from sweet white locally grown and late-harvested grapes—usually Lambrusco or Trebbiano varieties—is cooked over a direct flame until concentrated by roughly half, then left to ferment naturally for up to three weeks. Next, it is matured and further concentrated for a minimum of twelve years in a "batteria," or five or more successively smaller aging barrels. These barrels are made of different types of wood, such as oak, chestnut, cherry, juniper, and mulberry, so that the vinegar can take on the complex flavours of the casks. Once a year, the vinegar is bottled from the smallest cask in the sequence. Each cask is then topped up with vinegar from the next cask up, with the largest cask getting filled with the new yield. None of the casks are ever completely drained. This aging process is similar to the solera process used for fine sherries, ports, sweet wines, and Spanish brandies. The vinegar gets thicker and more concentrated as it ages because of evaporation that occurs

through the walls of the barrels—the vinegar in the smallest barrel will be much thicker and more syrupy than the liquid in the successively larger barrels.

After browsing through some different balsamic vinegars at the stall, I decided that even though there was a wide selection to choose from, I'd buy the one that I'd tasted first. I beamed, my confidence restored because I was certain I could cook something with it. As we left the stall, I turned to my wife and asked what she wanted to eat for dinner.

"I want beef steak today. Also, some fresh vegetables. It's been awhile since the last time we ate a good vegetable dish."

Frida accompanied me to the supermarket. Although confident in my cooking abilities, in the moment I still wasn't certain what to make using our new vinegar. But I knew that my wife always loved salad with balsamic vinegar, so I asked her to find me the salad ingredients that she likes. I watched with pride as she examined vegetables for freshness. How far we'd come! Catching me looking, Frida smiled, a smile that lit up my world, making my heart glow with love for my beautiful, caring wife. It was obvious she was as invested in the meal as I was, choosing vegetables for us with the same passion with

which I cooked for her. I left her in the produce aisle as I went to find some other ingredients.

Frida met me at the butcher's counter, presenting me with what she'd found. "I think I want to eat a very simple salad today. So I picked out the nicest lettuce and the plumpest tomatoes."

While she'd been gone, I had chosen a good beef for the steak. She squeezed my arm and nodded her approval as the butcher wrapped our meat.

Not all steaks are created equal. Many kinds of cuts of beef at the supermarket have the word "steak" in their names, but beware. Chuck steak, blade steak, round steak, tip steak, or even sirloin steak are not the best steaks, in my opinion. Rather, I've found that if it has the word rib, or loin, or strip in its name, it's going to make a good steak. Trust your recipe, but if in doubt, go for these cuts of beef.

That day, I chose rib-eye steak. My mouth already watered as I imagined my steak coupled with Frida's simple salad.

As I continued to browse through the store, hunting down more ingredients to use in my meal, my wife said, "I'm so hungry!

If you don't mind, I think I will buy some food for lunch while waiting for you to finish shopping."

She left and I continued searching for *something*… I wasn't sure what and a lack of confidence bloomed in me again. Normally an ingredient will stand out to me and I'll know what I want to cook. That hadn't happened yet. I still didn't know what, exactly, to make for dinner. Steak and salad, yes, but what did I want to do with these parts to make a whole, pleasing meal? It didn't feel special enough to merely grill the steak and serve it with a side salad.

My brow furrowed in deep thought. I noticed Frida enjoying her lunch at a sandwich stall. Calling out, I asked, "What are you eating for lunch? It looks nice."

Holding up her food, she replied, "It's a sandwich of thinly sliced, cold sausages and honey mustard sauce."

Aha! Suddenly an idea popped into my mind, and I knew just what I wanted to cook.

"Is it okay for me to cook another sandwich for you tonight? With steak and my version of honey mustard?"

"Of course. I never get tired of eating anything with honey mustard sauce."

Inspired, I grabbed some other ingredients, such as honey, Dijon mustard, olive oil, flat bread, and chicken eggs. I remembered that my wife loved the coriander—also known as cilantro—and onion I used to complement my guacamole. So I would reuse those two ingredients too. As I picked up some garlic, rosemary, and butter for frying the steak, I recalled what Ina Garten had said:

"Gardens look better when they are created by loving gardeners rather than by landscapers, because the garden is more tended to and cared for. The same thing goes for cooking."

This meal would be my garden. Having paid attention to what my wife loved to eat most, I knew my recipe was based in love. And with love as its primary ingredient, I didn't believe any meal could fail.

Since I'd decided to make a sauce with the balsamic vinegar that I bought, and I knew how important texture was to marrying ingredients, I also needed to get something to make my sauce smoother. I found some olive oils with a wide range of quality. Strangely, the shelf was quite full, as if not many people had been buying olive oil for their cooking. Perhaps, I thought, because so many people have misconceptions about Extra Virgin Olive Oil (EVOO), they are confused about all the ways we can use it in our food.

Some people may be concerned that EVOO is too expensive to be used daily. But what if we think about it in a different way? EVOO is a primary component of a Mediterranean diet, proven healthy for centuries, with hundreds of scientific studies conducted over the last 60 years to back it up. Furthermore, the taste of olive oil enhances the food flavour. So while it is true that the commonly used vegetable and seed oils cost much less than extra virgin olive oil, the benefits of EVOO outweigh the difference in cost from traditional cooking oil. I was cooking for my lovely wife and, as such, I was responsible for her well-being and pleasure. I had to choose the better—if more expensive—oil.

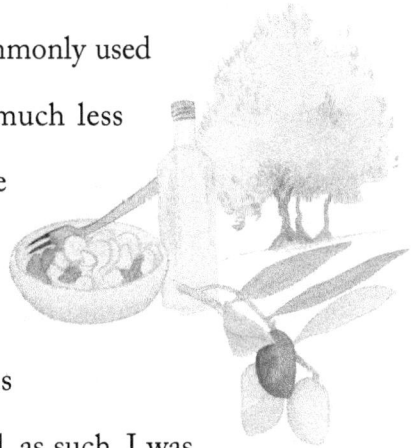

I love what one of my friends shared with me, saying, "Small little things make a big difference! The cooking oil we use to prepare meals is that small little thing. Next time we are eating out or in, we might pause and wonder how our meal will influence our health later. What will happen when we reach fifty years old if we're taking in small little doses of cooking oil from the food we consume every day?"

This convinced me to use olive oil rather than one of the cheaper oils for my cooking. And EVOO is the highest quality olive oil, extracted from olives through a process called cold pressing, which means the oil was removed using only pressure, and it was not heated over a certain temperature. This is the best way to keep all of the good-for-you antioxidants and monounsaturated fats in the oil. Cold pressing also preserves the most olive flavour and keeps the acidity under one percent. Finally, EVOO has a "low smoke point," which means it doesn't take a high temperature for it to start smoking. This would give it a stronger taste when I cooked with it. With all of these considerations in mind, I was certain EVOO would be the best option for my sauce.

After a few more hours strolling through the mall, we finally

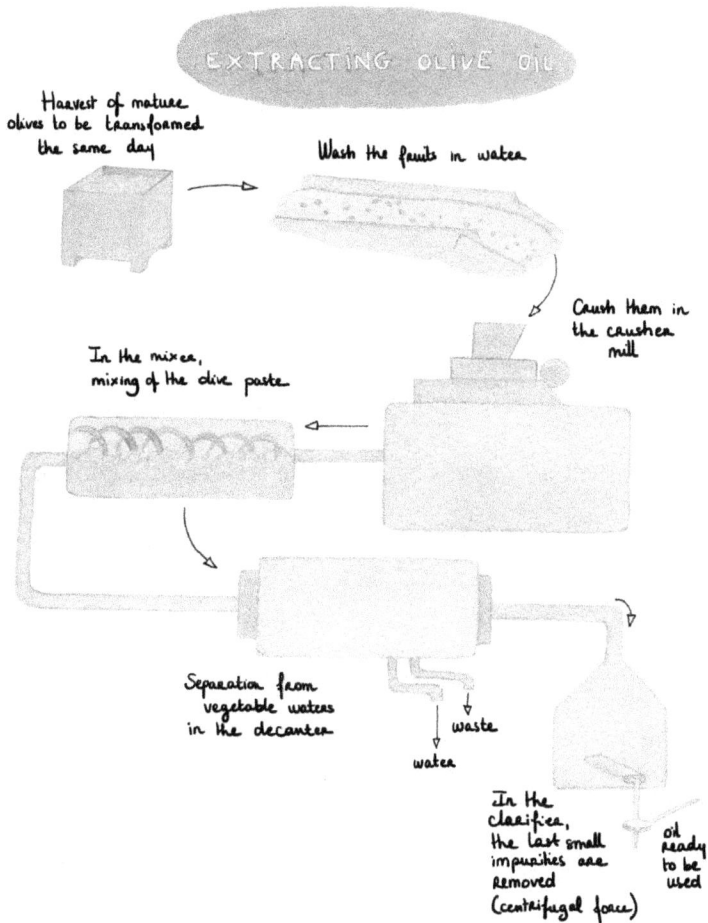

EXTRACTING OLIVE OIL

Harvest of mature olives to be transformed the same day

Wash the fruits in water

Crush them in the crusher mill

In the mixer, mixing of the olive paste

Separation from vegetable waters in the decanter

waste water

In the clarifier, the last small impurities are removed (centrifugal force)

oil ready to be used

decided to go home. It was already close to dinnertime when we got there. Going right to the kitchen, I started to prepare sandwiches for the two of us.

I created the sauce mixture first because it would need time to combine and create the best taste. I used one egg yolk, one teaspoon of Dijon mustard, two teaspoons of honey, and three teaspoons of balsamic vinegar. Then I stirred the mixture while slowly adding the olive oil, stopping when the mixture had become runny and smooth (about one cup of EVOO).

I seasoned the steak with salt and pepper, making sure that it was at room temperature. Then I pan-fried it with one head of crushed garlic, butter, and one sprig of rosemary. I used a large spoon to slowly scoop up the hot oil in the frying pan and poured it over and over on top of the steak being cooked. This cooked the outer side of the steak while keeping the inner part of it slightly raw.

When my steak was cooked, I let it rest for about 10 minutes. Letting a steak "rest" makes it tender and juicy when one cuts it later. While waiting for the steak to rest, I grabbed the pita bread, which usually comes in an ellipse or round shape, and pan fried it without using any oil—just enough to warm it up and make it crispy. After frying the bread, I sliced it in half and I opened it up to form a pocket.

By then, the steak had sufficiently rested, and I thinly sliced the meat. Lastly, I put it all together in a pita bread pocket with one layer of vegetables cut in strips lining the bottom of the pocket, followed by one tablespoon of my balsamic honey

STEAK WRAP

Make a sauce with

1 egg yolk

1 teaspoon of Dijon mustard

2 teaspoons of honey

3 teaspoons of balsamic vinegar

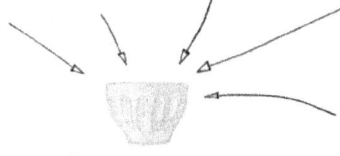

olive oil (about 1 cup)

Stir until it becomes runny and smooth

Season the steak with

salt & pepper

and fry it with

1 head of crushed garlic

butter

1 sprig of rosemary

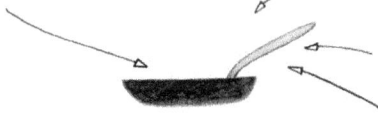

Scoop up the hot butter and pour it on top of the steak over and over again.

Let the steak rest for about 10 minutes

Fry the pita bread

and slice it in half

Open the bread to form a pocket and put in

strip lining vegetables

1 tbsp of sauce

thinly sliced steak

coriander

another tbsp of sauce

mustard sauce, then sliced steak, and finally topped it all off with coriander and another tablespoon of the sauce.

I used pita bread instead of loaf bread for my sandwich because Frida had already had a regular bread sandwich for lunch. I didn't want to bore her with a meal too similar to what she had just eaten. Furthermore, pita bread makes a tasty wrap, which bound all my flavours together well.

Once everything was done, I called, "The dinner is ready."

My face glowed with pride and my heart with warmth. Just letting Frida know that dinner is ready has come to mean so much to me. It is a privilege to say that to someone you love. I know she feels she has received special treatment whenever I tell her I've cooked for her and it is ready because she knows the care I've put into her health and pleasure.

We enjoyed our sandwiches very much that night.

Frida complimented me between bites, saying, "Now we've found the sourness *and* the sweetness we've been looking for!

This is so refreshing and appetizing. I love it! Thank you, Beib!"

And although it contained steak, the meal was also a successful vegetable dish that Frida and even I—not much of a vegetable lover—liked very much, thanks to the organic produce Frida had chosen at the market. The plump tomatoes and the crunch from the lettuce added another dimension of texture to my dish, and, all in all, the vegetables were refreshing and cool, a delightful complement to the warm, tender steak.

We ate while watching some educational TV shows. Coincidentally, a reporter mentioned that after reviewing 343 studies on organic produce, researchers in Europe and the United States concluded that organic crops and organic-crop-based foods contained higher concentrations of antioxidants on average than conventionally grown foods. At the same time, the researchers found that conventional foods contained greater concentrations of residual pesticides and the toxic metal cadmium.

ORGANIC FARM

"This shows clearly that organically grown fruits, vegetables, and grains deliver tangible nutrition and

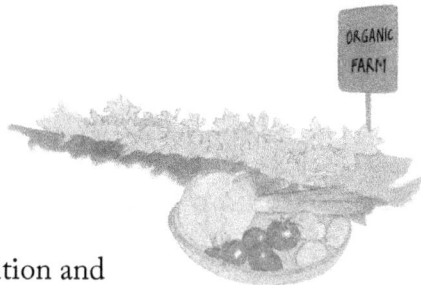

food safety benefits," said study co-author Charles Benbrook, a research professor at Washington State University's Centre for Sustaining Agriculture and Natural Resources.

Our eyes met upon hearing this news. "Thanks to you, I already knew that organic vegetables made the best choice for your cooking," Frida said. "Now I know it's not just because they taste better. They are also healthier."

Smiling with pride, I got up and brought back some more of the vegetables we'd bought that afternoon. I ate the leftover vegetables with relish, even without steak and pita—just plain.

Frida laughed. "This is the first time I've ever seen you eat that many vegetables!"

"Thanks to that show reporter," I said with a grin, "and to your good choices."

That night it was as if a burden had been lifted. I no longer had an issue with all kinds of sourness. Whenever my wife craved something sour, I now knew that I could create something using traditional balsamic vinegar.

Seeking the best way to combine the new taste of balsamic vinegar with flavours familiar to me has been an inspiring journey. And it hasn't been only about the food I cook. Rather, this journey represents my effort to accept and honour different cultures and upbringings. Learning to respect others' experiences has enhanced all aspects of my life and certainly my relationships.

Cooking for my loved ones has taught me so much! I've learned that it's all right to lack confidence in the kitchen. It's all right to start out knowing little about food and how to prepare it. I've come to believe that we don't even have to love to cook to become skilled at it. We only need to cook for the ones we love. The rest will follow.

In times of doubt, I remember the steak wrap and this reassures me that all cooking, like life, is a journey. And mine has only just begun. I still become discouraged at times, lacking the confidence or will to continue on the right path toward love and communication. Sometimes I simply feel unmotivated to go on, either because of recent failures and difficulties, or even just because I am tired. But fond memories of cooking for my wife—and for my other loved ones—bolsters my confidence, gives me strength and hope, and the will to continue my journey.

As you may recall, it was memories of my father that started me on this voyage of self-discovery and growth through cooking for my loved ones. Often, remembering this great man still

motivates me. I recently remembered a defining moment for me, from just before my father passed away, when he was still in the hospital, a time when I was able to prepare the right meal for him…

After moving to Singapore, before my father got very sick, I used to dream about cooking my best recipes for him. Yet my dreams never came to fruition, as I always made excuses when I saw him. I told myself that there would be more time on the next visit—during the next Christmas, the next New Year, the next Chinese New Year, and so on.

At the time, I'd forgotten about his omelette, created out of love for me. I'd forgotten many of our happy times together. Thus, instead of treating him with love and respect, I quarrelled with him often.

Looking back, I see the part I had in those fights. I thought at the time that I was old enough and had more knowledge in life, believed I knew better, and never paused to consider his perspective, never put myself in his shoes. Perhaps these disagreements with my father reminded me too much of how he used to fight with my mother, or maybe the real problem was shame over my own mistakes, manifested as anger and intolerance.

Whatever the root cause, I chose not to remember the good life my father had provided me, and our relationship became soured by miscommunication and poor judgment. So when I visited, I never felt inspired to cook for him. Ma even suggested once that I have a nice talk with my father over a dinner that I prepared. But I ignored her. Without remembering how my father used to express his love for me by cooking, I did not yet believe in the power of cooking for one's loved ones.

However, now that I *do* believe, I often think back to my last dinner with my father when I am in need of motivation to cook for my loved ones.

It was May, 2012. I'd travelled home to visit my father in the hospital after the surgery on his elbow. An infection in his bones following surgery gave my father a great deal of pain. Doctors had given my father a lot of pain medication and he could not eat. I remember how pale and thin he was, propped up on pillows, unable to get out of bed.

After two days of no appetite, my father was taken off pain medication in the hope that he'd eat something. My mother and sister had gone to take care of some things, leaving me alone with my father.

Swallowing my tears, I tried to be strong for him. "What do you want to eat?" I asked. "You must eat, Pa."

His thin shoulders went up in an attempt to shrug. "Anything will do," he told me.

Yet his dinner tray remained untouched. My heart ached to see his dry lips, his sunken cheeks. "The nurse brought you dinner," I said, hopefully.

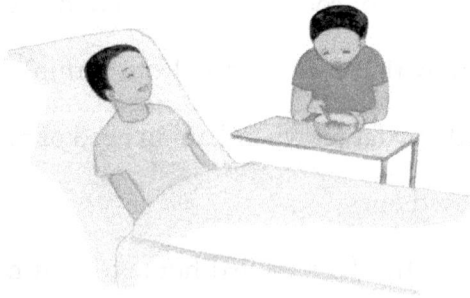

My father's eyes fell on the tray, but he made no move to eat. My desperation brought on a sudden inspiration and I said, "How about I prepare this for you in a way you'll like?"

He didn't have to explain to me how he'd like it. I remembered how my father liked his food—how dry, how soupy, how sweet, how salty, and so on, because our family had often eaten our meals together when I was growing up. Knowing how to prepare food for my father later in his life showed me the power and importance of family gathering together at the same table for meals.

When my father nodded his willingness to try the food I prepared, I examined the dinner the nurse had brought. First, I noted how dry the rice and vegetables looked. But there was some chicken broth on the tray, and I remembered how much my father used to like mixing his rice with soup. Pouring the chicken broth into the rice, I then mixed in the vegetables, finally stirring it all together until the rice and vegetables were soft and fragrant. My father smiled but was too weak to hold a spoon by himself, so I fed him, one spoonful at a time.

The food began to perk him up and between bites, my father talked about his old friends, about our neighbours, about how he'd struggled when I was young, and then, also, how happy he'd always felt when he cooked for me. That night, over dinner in the hospital, was the first time I'd had a good talk with my father in years.

"This food is nice. You prepared it well, and just how I wanted it to be," he said.

Pride swelled in my chest. All that shame and regret I'd been feeling fell away, leaving behind confidence and love.

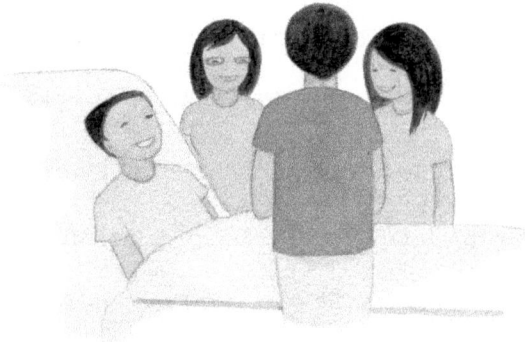

After dinner ended, my mom and sister returned, and we talked even more together. That night I promised myself that I'd cook a proper meal for my father after he was discharged from the hospital.

I slept peacefully, certain that everything would be all right soon. And the next day, though my father was not ready to go home yet, I flew back to Singapore still believing that everything would be all right. I would cook for my father the next time I saw him.

Unfortunately, that time never came. As I wrote previously,

one night, my mother called to inform me that my father had passed away. I was devastated, not only by my loss, but also because I'd thought that I would have another opportunity to cook him a meal and to have another nice chat with him.

After my father's passing, I had to accept that this dream would never come true. The best I can do now is cook in his memory, serving loved ones a meal in front of my father's photo whenever I visit my hometown, without the chance to see him smile while enjoying my food.

Some people say, "Tomorrow might be too late," but to me even *tonight* might be too late. I hope, dear readers that you will learn from my mistake…

So what are you waiting for? Get up and go to your kitchen and cook something—anything—for your loved ones. It can be something from your memory about your childhood or perhaps something from this book, or you might even recreate a salad that you have been eating while you've been reading… What you prepare, the meal you create, does not have to be fancy. It only has to be *now*.

So go, and start on your own cooking journey! Cook through disappointment and regret, through miscommunication and poor judgment, through lack of confidence and insecurity. Walk through your kitchen as you walk through life: with courage, joy, honour, and friendship in your heart.

And remember, home cooking is the true embodiment of love because it makes us show patience, kindness, humility, hope, and perseverance.

Agus & Father

About the Authors

AGUS EKANURDI AND FRIDA ANTONY have been happily married since 2011, and *Cook Your Way to Love & Harmony* is their first book. They began working on *Cook Your Way to Love & Harmony* in 2015, to honor Agus's father, So Kong Hoo, who passed away in 2012. So Kong Hoo taught Agus how to improve relationships and lead a healthier, more loving life by cooking for one's loved ones. By sharing recipes and relating the true stories of their own experiences, Agus and Frida hope that this book will inspire readers to cook for their loved ones and show readers how to improve their relationships through communication, friendship, and, of course, home cooking.

Agus and Frida currently live in Singapore with their young son, Philip Su. Their next book will be about cooking for their son and other parenting experiences. In the future, they hope to explore the world together—learning about new cuisines—and to carry on the legacy of improving relationships through cooking to the next generation.

You can find out more about Agus & Frida on their website at AgusFrida.com.

www.ingramcontent.com/pod-product-compliance
Lightning Source LLC
Chambersburg PA
CBHW060920040426
42445CB00011B/713